Motivation and Emotion

Motivation and Emotion provides an explanation of emotional experience and aspects of human behaviour using psychological, physiological and alternative approaches. The brain mechanisms that govern motivations are discussed and questions such as 'Why don't we eat ourselves to death?' and 'How do we know we are thirsty?' are answered.

Phil Gorman is an A-level teacher at Stafford College, UK, and a chief examiner for the Edexcel A Level Examination Board.

Routledge Modular Psychology

Series editors: Cara Flanagan is a Reviser for AS and A2 level Psychology and an experienced teacher and examiner. Philip Banyard is Associate Senior Lecturer in Psychology at Nottingham Trent University and a Chief Examiner for AS and A2 level Psychology.

The *Routledge Modular Psychology* series is a completely new approach to introductory-level psychology, tailor-made to the new modular style of teaching. Each short book covers a topic in more detail than any large textbook can, allowing teacher and student to select material exactly to suit any particular course or project.

The books have been written especially for those students new to higher-level study, whether at school, college or university. They include specially designed features to help with technique, such as a model essay at an average level with an examiner's comments to show how extra marks can be gained. The authors are all examiners and teachers at the introductory level.

The *Routledge Modular Psychology* texts are all user-friendly and accessible and use the following features:

- practice essays with specialist commentary to show how to achieve a higher grade
- chapter summaries to assist with revision
- progress and review exercises
- glossary of key terms
- summaries of key research
- further reading to stimulate ongoing study and research
- cross-referencing to other books in the series

For more details on our AS, A2 and *Routledge Modular Psychology* publications visit our website at www.a-levelpsychology.co.uk

Also available in this series (titles listed by syllabus section):

Michelle, Dale, Hayley and
'Stan' for everything

For Chris Gorman 'Dad' (1924–2003)

Motivation and Emotion

Phil Gorman

Routledge
Taylor & Francis Group

LONDON AND NEW YORK

First published 2004
by Routledge
27 Church Road, Hove, East Sussex BN3 2FA

Simultaneously published in the USA and Canada
by Routledge
29 West 35th Street, New York NY 10001

Routledge is an imprint of the Taylor & Francis Group

© 2004 Phil Gorman

Typeset in Times and Frutiger by Keystroke,
Jacaranda Lodge, Wolverhampton
Printed and bound in Great Britain by
TJ International Ltd, Padstow, Cornwall
Paperback cover design by Anú Design

This publication has been produced with paper manufactured to strict
environmental standards and with pulp derived from sustainable forests.

British Library Cataloguing in Publication Data
A catalogue record for this book is available from the British Library

Library of Congress Cataloging-in-Publication Data
Gorman, Phil, 1965–
  Motivation and emotion / Phil Gorman.–1st ed.
    p. cm. — (Routledge modular psychology series)
  Includes bibliographical references and index.
  ISBN 0-415-22770-4 — ISBN 0-415-22769-0 (pbk.)
  1. Motivation (Psychology) 2. Motivation
(Psychology)–Physiological
aspects. 3. Emotions. 4. Emotions–Physiological aspects.
I. Title. II. Series: Routledge modular psychology.
  BF503.G67 2003
  153.8—dc22

                                                        2003014341

                                        ISBN 0-415-22769-0 (hbk)
                                        ISBN 0-415-22770-4 (pbk)

Contents

Illustrations

Figures

Tables

Introduction

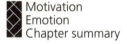

Motivation
Emotion
Chapter summary

Motivation

In many ways the study of motivation is the study of psychology itself. It is concerned with explaining all forms of behaviour, from why you have decided to study psychology, to why some people take up bungee-jumping.

Motivation is an attempt to explain the 'why' of behaviour.

Essentially, when we ask why a person or animal acts in a particular way, we are asking about their motivation (Mook, 1996).

When an actor is asked by a director to act in a particular way, the actor may ask, 'What is my motivation?' The actor needs to know the reason for an action in order to be able to perform it properly, just as you may need a reason to continue with your studies or even to carry on reading this book.

Motivation is concerned with goal-directed behaviour, what it is that pushes us towards certain forms of behaviour and not others. On the one hand, your reason for reading this book may be purely functional i.e. it will help you pass your exam. On the other hand, your reason may be more personal e.g. to help understand some aspect of your own behaviour or those around you. Whatever the reason, the issues covered in this book will hopefully help you do both of the above.

Some of the issues covered in the chapters of this book are:

Why do some people eat more than others? (Chapter 3)

Why do we have a preference for certain types of food? (Chapter 3)

What makes us start and stop drinking? (Chapter 4)

What is the attraction of alcohol? (Chapter 4)

What is the difference between high and low achievers? (Chapter 5)

Why do some people have the drive to become top athletes? (Chapter 5)

What is it that makes us avoid unpleasant situations? (Chapter 6)

Why do some (strange) people engage in ridiculously dangerous activities? (Chapter 6)

These and other issues will be explained through an emphasis on the interaction between internal and external factors in the determination of our behaviour; this interaction will help us to understand the behaviours outlined above.

Therefore, the book will concern itself with the physiological processes involved in bringing about changes in behaviour, in particular, autonomic reactions involved in maintaining a stable internal environment (**homeostasis**). But, it will also concern itself with the complex mental processes involved in making an assessment of a particular external situation, before deciding how to act.

As stated above, motivation is concerned with the complex processes that move individuals towards some goal, to try and understand the forces that push them into action. The idea of forces pushing us into action is generally linked to the notion of biological drives and instincts, which compel us to adopt certain forms of behaviour. However, if we see motivation as involving mental processes then it appears to be linked more closely to cognitive factors, which involve a logical assessment of the situation before we decide to act.

Whilst it may be biological drives that cause us to pull back from the edge of a cliff when we get too close, there must be other factors involved in our decision to throw ourselves off the top of a bridge with nothing but a piece of elastic tied to our leg.

Theories of motivation

Theories of motivation centre on three distinct but often interrelated concepts:

- instinct/drive
- incentive
- arousal

Most explanations of motivated behaviour will make some reference to one or other of these three.

Each of these will help to explain the main types of motives, which have been identified by psychologists:

1. An instinctive desire to satisfy a specific physiological need or drive. For example, consider the role of physiological drives in relation to eating and drinking:

    How do you know when you are hungry/thirsty?
    How do you decide when to eat/drink?
    How do you know when you have had enough?

According to this approach the answers to all of these questions are physiological and concerned with purely physiological responses e.g. stomach contractions.

In Chapters 3 and 4 we will consider the extent to which it is possible to answer these questions in purely physiological terms.

2. A decision to act in a particular way in order to gain satisfaction or reward. For example, consider the role of rewards in relation to work:

    What is it that makes you work hard at a particular job?

According to this approach, the only incentive to work hard is the expectation of some future reward (pay, praise etc.).

In Chapter 5 we will assess this possibility in relation to psychological theories of motivation.

3. The desire to increase or decrease one's level of arousal. For example, consider the role of arousal in relation to going on holiday:

> Why is it that some people choose extremely adventurous holidays, whilst others just go on holiday to relax?

This approach combines the desire for changes in your physiological state with individual differences in psychological assessment of the situation to explain these behaviours.

The actor's question, 'What's my motivation?' seems to be rather more difficult to answer than we might have first thought and perhaps the only person who can answer that question is the actor him/herself.

Emotion

What are emotions?

If someone were to come up to you now and say, 'How do you feel?' What would you say?

You might refer to your physical state, but you might be just as likely to reply with some reference to your emotional state. For example, 'I'm happy enough', or 'I'm fed up/bored'. Both of these examples can be applied to those things we call emotions.

Whilst these two may not be the first things that come to mind when we consider what emotions are, they would almost certainly fall into the category of emotion.

At this point you may well be expecting some form of definition of what an emotion is. Unfortunately, the situation is not that simple and there have been many attempts to come to an agreed definition of emotions, none of which has so far proved satisfactory. Chapter 7 of this book will look at some of these attempts and consider the possibility of coming to a universal definition of certain emotions. It will also try to identify the physiological factors involved in the production of an emotion, just where do emotions come from?

Let us just say for the moment that emotions involve some appraisal of inner thoughts, feelings and memories, sometimes combined with an assessment of the environment and physiological changes, most often involving a behavioural response (Kleinginna and Kleinginna, 1981).

Consider the emotion of fear, this will often involve:

- An assessment of a particular situation.
- An appraisal of our memory will provide a clue as to whether or not the situation is dangerous.
- This will be followed by a cognitive appraisal of our thoughts about the situation; physiological responses (such as increased heart rate) will guide our feelings.
- This will lead to a behavioural response i.e. running away.

Using the previous example as a guide, come up with your own list of emotions, which would fit into these criteria. Are there any other things that do not fit but you would count as emotions? Make a list of those too. Now create one list of emotions in the form of a 'top ten' that represent what you think are the clearest/best examples of emotions.

Progress exercise

One attempt to provide such a list was carried out by Fehr and Russell (1984), who interviewed 200 Canadian college students and asked them to rate a list of words in order from a very good example of an emotion to a very poor one. The results are shown in Table 1.1.

Theories of emotion

It is one thing to be able to identify an emotion, but it is somewhat more complicated to explain what it is that brings about the physical changes that are usually associated with an emotional state (facial expressions, sweating etc.).

Each of the theories that follows provides some combination of the four factors identified above; feelings, bodily reactions, appraisal of environmental stimuli and behaviour. Each one provides some combination of a scenario involving a *stimulus* (the sight of a bear or ferocious dog), *feelings* (I'm scared), *bodily reactions* (increased heart rate or muscle tension) and *behaviour* (running away or playing dead) – [bears can run really fast]. Essentially the theories can be broken

Table 1.1 Students' 'top ten' emotions

1.	Happiness (152)	
2.	Anger (149)	Do these examples fit with your own 'top ten'?
3.	Sadness (136)	Consider any differences between your list and this one. Why might that be? Most of the emotions mentioned here are negative.
4.	Love (124)	
5.	Fear (96)	
6.	Hate (89)	Why do you think that is? Is there something more powerful about these emotions that causes them to be remembered better than positive ones?
7.	Joy (82)	
8.	Excitement (53)	
9.	Anxiety (50)	
10.	Depression (42)	

(The numbers in brackets show how many students chose that particular example.)

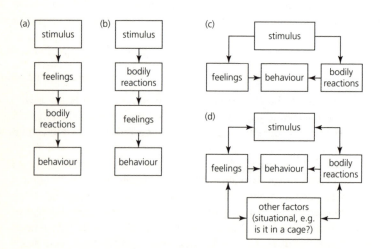

Figure 1.1 Four representations of the sequence of emotional activity

down into three patterns or sequences of activity, which could be shown up against what might be seen as the common-sense view of emotional experience (Figure 1.1).

Progress exercise

Which of the four representations fits best with your own experience?

Which one makes the most common sense?

(a) Represents the view that emotions begin with the subjective feeling (fear), which in turn leads to physiological changes (increased heart rate), followed by an appropriate behaviour (running away).
(b) Represents the view that emotions begin with physiological changes, which cause the subjective feeling of fear.
(c) Represents the view that physiological changes and subjective feelings occur simultaneously.
(d) Represents the view that the whole process is far more complex than the other sequential representations suggest. The process should be seen as an interaction between cognitive factors, the environment and the nervous system. All of which will have an effect on our behaviour, in ways that are far from predictable or sequential.

Consider, for example, the experience of taking exams (a common experience for most students). These theories will provide very different explanations for the emotions exhibited by each student:

(a) If the student has not prepared well for the exam, this will cause them to worry about the exam, which could lead to physical reactions, sweating, raised heartbeat, general anxiety. All of this could have effects on their performance in the exam.
(b) The student notices that some of the physical changes mentioned above are happening as they get closer to doing the exam. This

causes the student to wonder what the cause of these changes might be leading to either feelings of worry and fear and consequent effects on performance.

(c) The student is feeling worried and afraid at the same time as experiencing these physical changes leading to affects on performance.

(d) This rather more complex approach suggests that the behaviour of the student will be influenced by their cognitive appraisal of these feelings and physical changes. The student may well feel physically aroused when approaching the exam, but may interpret this arousal as excitement rather than fear, due to their long hours of preparation and confidence in their ability. Such an appraisal will have an effect on their behaviour, which in this instance is likely to be more positive than the other three explanations suggest.

Chapter 8 of this book will consider these theories in more detail (in relation to other emotions as well as fear), and assess the role of thoughts in the experience of emotion. Why is it that some people experience stronger emotions than others in response to the same stimulus?

Chapter summary

Motivation deals with the causes of people's behaviour, it attempts to explain why we behave in the way that we do. In order to understand motivation properly, an assessment of internal, physiological needs and external, situational demands must be made. Theories of motivation try to explain our behaviour with reference to instincts and drives, incentives and rewards, and the desire to change one's level of arousal. These theories have been applied to fairly mundane activities such as eating and drinking, as well as to more adventurous activities, such as bungee-jumping.

Emotion has proved very difficult to define, partly because emotions are not easy to identify, and partly because the feeling and expression of emotion is so relative.

An agreed list of emotions that are common to all individuals is very difficult to create. Theories of emotion combine the appraisal of a stimulus, the feeling of being scared, physiological reactions and behaviour in order to explain the emotional experience. Unfortunately, they all do it in slightly different ways, so that there is no agreement over which of these comes first, or indeed if any one of them comes before the others.

Further reading

Green, S. (1994) *Principles of Biopsychology*. Hove/Hillsdale, NJ: Lawrence Erlbaum Associates. As the title suggests this is a very useful introduction to the main principles of biopsychology, which contains chapters on the nervous system, motivation and emotion.

The physiological approach to motivation

■ Physiological theories of motivation
◇ Physiological drives
▨ Homeostatic drive theory
▲ Chapter summary

Physiological theories of motivation

Instinct theory

In a book of this sort it is probably not worth spending too long considering the evolutionary basis of animal and human behaviour, particularly as it is covered in other titles in this series, and other books have considered these issues with much more relevance than would be possible here (Colgan, 1989; Wong, 2000). This theory stems from Darwin's theory of **evolution** as set out in *The Origin of Species* (Darwin, 1859).

Darwin suggests that we are born with instincts, which push us towards certain forms of behaviour. The most basic of these behaviours is the instinct to survive. This instinct will prevail at all costs, obviously, without it we would not survive.

All behaviour can be seen therefore in the light of this basic overriding concern – sex, eating, drinking, sleeping, etc.

This approach has gained respectability in the past (early 20th century), due to the work of Darwin in suggesting the close relationship between humans and animals. If this relationship is as historically similar, as Darwin suggests, then all of our behaviour will be guided by this one overriding concern. If not then our behaviour must be driven by other forces.

Instinct theory has proved to be problematic in genetic terms for biologists and psychologists alike, but may prove to be more problematic for the study of motivated behaviour.

Whilst instincts do help us to understand basic/early motivated behaviours, they do not help us to understand the more complex human activities of art or culture, for example. If we are going to understand this type of behaviour then we would need to develop more instincts than just those that are directly related to survival. There are clearly a number of behaviours that separate us from animals, which we may consider to be driven by these more basic instincts. In fact the phrases that we use to describe people who display these kind of instinctive behaviours reflect our attitude towards them.

eating like a . . .
drinks like a . . .
fight like . . .
breeds like a . . .

These phrases are often used in an offensive way to suggest that our behaviour as humans should be somewhat different from animals that are after all controlled by little more than their instincts to do some of the above.

This process is often taken further though by phrases that suggest the need to separate mature humans from their immature counterparts with phrases such as 'crying like a baby'.

This phrase may actually help to provide some support for instinct theory. It suggests that humans may be dominated by their instincts in their early years, but that these instincts are either socialised out of us or that we are taught, as adults, to hide them better than children are apparently able to do.

These points still do not solve the problem of the need to identify more than just physiological instincts for both animals and children.

In order to do this we need to identify a list of instincts, which could explain all human behaviour.

How many instincts?

Try to create your own list of instincts. You might consider dividing them into *biological* and *psychological* instincts:

Biological   **Psychological**

Progress exercise

The first attempt at this was made by William James (1890), who tried to relate these instincts directly to their evolutionary past by studying his own children (Table 2.1). He suggested that humans are *more* strongly influenced by instincts because we are influenced by psychological as well as biological ones.

Since then further attempts have been made to develop such a list e.g. McDougall (1908) developed a list of 12 instincts (Table 2.1), these were basic instincts and made little reference to specifically psychosocial motives and therefore further lists were needed. McClelland (1961) used the same kind of basic instincts but added further ones that were related to certain **needs,** for example the need for achievement, and the need for affiliation (Table 2.1).

Unfortunately, attempts at producing lists of this sort caused more problems than they solved, as more lists were produced so more instincts were recognised as being in need of inclusion. Around 15,000 instincts have been identified over the years, and if this many have been identified there are probably more that have still not been identified yet. In more recent times instincts have become redundant in attempts to *explain* motivated behaviour, as they have become little more than just meaningless labels.

Physiological drives

A possible biological alternative to the notion of instincts in determining behaviour comes from the study of 'drives'. This has a long history in psychology and is not confined to purely biological explanations/theories.

Table 2.1 **Three attempts to produce a list of instincts**

James (1890)	McDougall (1908)	McClelland (1961)
Anger	Escape	McClelland used the same basic instincts identified so far and applied them to important individual needs. Particularly important were the need for achievement, the need for affiliation and the need for power.
Fear	Combat	
Hunting	Repulsion	
Acquisitiveness	Protectiveness	
Constructiveness	Mating	
Sympathy	Food-seeking	
Imitation	Hoarding	
Play	Submission	
Curiosity	Assertion	
Sociability	Curiosity	
Cleanliness	Construction	
Modesty/Shame	Gregariousness	
Love		

As an explanation of the biological basis of behaviour, drives take us into the cellular and neurochemical areas of physiology. A drive is determined by certain tissue needs and is satisfied through the activation of brain receptors leading to the release of hormones. Chapters 3 and 4 will look at the influence of these factors on the motivational states of hunger and thirst (widely recognised as the most basic and fundamental of physiological drives).

An understanding of these drives and others, such as temperature regulation and sex, require an understanding of central and autonomic nervous system operations, which maintain normal functioning through homeostatic regulation of the endocrine system.

The structure of the nervous system

The neuron

The nervous system is made up of billions of cells called **neurons**, which have the ability to transmit electrical impulses. It is through this transmission of electrical impulses that each neuron is able to pass messages to and from the brain indicating what action is required, or indeed if no action is required.

Central and peripheral nervous system

The brain and the spinal cord make up the **central nervous system** (CNS), which is the master control system for all actions and reactions in the body. The CNS is connected to the rest of the body through the **peripheral nervous system** (PNS), which consists of nerves that extend from the spinal cord to all parts of the body; each nerve is made up of a collection of neurons.

The brain dominates the nervous system and although it could be sub-divided into many hundreds of parts, for the purposes of this book, it is enough to say that the brain contains a number of areas that are believed to be directly responsible for certain forms of behaviour.

- The **raphe nuclei** and the **reticular formation** are both involved in arousal.
- The **hypothalamus** is involved in homeostatic regulation.
- The **cerebral cortex** controls higher cognitive functioning.
- The **limbic system** is involved in emotional control.

Autonomic nervous system

This is a branch of the PNS, which is directly involved in the maintenance of a stable internal state (**homeostasis**). The **autonomic nervous system** (ANS) transmits information to the organs, glands and smooth muscles involved in the regulation of the internal environment of the body (autonomic means self-regulating). Therefore, the ANS has a particularly important role in the control of motivational behaviours, such as eating and drinking, and emotional behaviours, such as '**fight or flight**' (Chapter 6).

The ANS has two components or branches; the *sympathetic and the para-sympathetic*, which have separate roles in this process but each controls the functioning of parts of the system to achieve stability. These branches are stimulated by sections of the brain and have a direct effect on all the major organs. For example, the heart will be made to beat faster in order to speed up the supply of oxygen. Table 2.2 shows the organs affected by the ANS and the different actions of the two branches upon them.

Table 2.2 Actions of the ANS		
Organ	**Sympathetic action**	**Parasympathetic action**
Eye	Dilates pupils	Constricts pupils
Mouth	Inhibits salivation	Stimulates salivation
Lungs	Relaxes airways	Constricts airways
Heart	Increases heart rate	Decreases heart rate
Sweat glands	Increases sweating	NO ACTION
Intestines	NO ACTION	Dilates blood vessels
Stomach	Inhibits digestion	Stimulates digestion
Liver	Stimulates glucose release	NO ACTION
Adrenal glands	Stimulates adrenaline release	NO ACTION
Skin	Constricts blood vessels	Dilates blood vessels
Bladder	Relaxes bladder	Contracts bladder
Penis	Stimulates ejaculation	Stimulates erection

Whilst the ANS involves a speedy and virtually automatic messenger system for homeostatic activity, the **endocrine system** is much slower and involves responses, which are stimulated by messengers in the blood stream (**hormones**). The release of hormones is controlled by the hypothalamus, which causes the release of hormones from various glands in the body; through the activation of the **pituitary** (master) **gland**. These systems are the basis for physiological explanations of motivated behaviours related to instincts and drives, which push the organism towards certain forms of behaviour in order to maintain normal homeostatic functioning.

Homeostatic drive theory

The notion that homeostatic drives determine our behaviour, was first put forward by Cannon (1929), who believed that the need to maintain a constant level of physiological functioning determines our behaviour.

In order to function normally our bodies have certain physiological needs that must be fulfilled, these include food, drink, sleep, warmth and shelter etc. When these needs have not been satisfied, physiological mechanisms are activated, which motivate us to restore this balance. The body's tendency to maintain a state of balance is called homeostasis. The most commonly used (and probably the most apt) analogy to explain the idea of homeostasis is the thermostat in a central-heating system. Like homeostasis, it is pre-set to a required level, it is sensitive to changes in the surrounding physical environment and it sends signals to the system to start/stop working as required. When a room falls below the set temperature, the thermostat will automatically turn on the heating system, when it goes up again the system will turn off, similarly when our body temperature rises and falls physiological mechanisms/behavioural responses will be triggered to return the required level.

The process is regulatory in that it involves responses that occur due to changes in the internal/external environment. These changes bring about an imbalance in the system, which must be resolved in order for the system to keep functioning properly. Some of these responses are automatic, as they do not require us to do anything in order to restore the balance. For example, when our body temperature rises, sweating will occur as a normal reaction of the ANS.

However, some changes require behavioural responses. For example, when the temperature drops we might rub our hands together to keep warm. At other times these changes will lead to both automatic and behavioural responses. For example, you could combine the behavioural response of removing an item of clothing with the automatic response of sweating to reduce your body temperature.

Progress exercise

Try to identify all of the possible physical and behavioural responses that a person could make to a rise/fall in body temperature (you might think about how you know you feel hot or cold and how you respond once you have realised).

Some of the main features of homeostasis have been outlined below:

- A **set point** identifies the ideal range for each component of the homeostatic mechanism.
- Each component has to have a *detector* to monitor the set-point maintenance.
- There must be a *correctional mechanism* to make alterations when the detectors register a significant deviation from the set point.
- As well as these reactive processes, which respond to physiological changes, there will also be a *prospective element* in homeostasis, which will help all animals to anticipate future changes that are likely to occur.

Temperature regulation

Set point

Whilst eating and drinking do not have an easily identifiable set point that must be maintained, body temperature does. We must try and maintain our core body temperature (blood temperature) at a relatively constant 37°C.

Detector

The hypothalamus is the main area of the brain involved in homeostasis and the area of the hypothalamus responsible for this detection is the preoptic area, which reacts to changes in its own temperature (Nelson and Prosser, 1981).

Control mechanism

If the preoptic area becomes cold, it stimulates the sympathetic branch of the ANS, which causes the blood vessels to constrict and thereby prevent the flow of warm blood to the surface of the skin where it would be cooled.

Other automatic reactions include piloerection, hairs on the skin rise to trap air and act as insulation (more commonly known as *goose-bumps*), and shivering.

All of these reactions serve to prevent heat being lost through the skin and thereby maintaining the core body temperature.

If the preoptic area becomes hot, the parasympathetic branch of the ANS causes the blood vessels to dilate, thereby releasing more warm blood to the surface. The sympathetic branch causes sweating to occur, which moistens the surface of the skin and keeps the whole body cool.

The prospective element

This aspect of temperature regulation is closely linked to the behavioural responses mentioned earlier. The system will act prospectively by behaving in ways that will prevent future changes in temperature, hunger or thirst causing us a problem.

For example, if we are setting out on a long walk on a warm (but probably cloudy) day, then we would top up our levels of food and water and probably take a coat along just in case. In this way we will not only prevent the possibility of thirst or hunger but also the likelihood of rain occurring and us getting cold.

Animals themselves engage in similar forms of behaviour (although most of them do not have the ability to remove their coats); large animals in hot countries with little rain will take on large amounts of water to prevent future dehydration. Animals will bury themselves in the ground to protect themselves from the extremes of hot and cold.

The extent to which these kinds of behaviour are still under the control of purely biological mechanisms is certainly open to question and in itself this kind of explanation only provides a small amount of the entire picture.

Evaluation

- The study of drives as the basis of motivated behaviour has received support from studies of hunger and thirst (see Chapters 3 and 4). The kind of set-point theory set out above may be even more convincing than these studies as the specific set point can be identified in temperature regulation in a way that is quite difficult with hunger and thirst.

  However, this approach has received criticism from a number of sides:

- The use of drives as an explanation tends to involve a circular argument. The theory seems to suggest that our behaviour is motivated by the drive and that we know that the drive exists because of the behaviour that precipitates it.
- Some reactions that maintain a homeostatic balance are automatic. It is fairly easy to understand the notion of behavioural drives in relation to eating, drinking and aspects of temperature regulation, but less so in relation to other homeostatic necessities such as breathing.
- Set-point theories of eating and drinking in particular do not support the evolutionary process mentioned above. Without the

prospective element of the homeostatic process mentioned above, it is almost impossible to understand how a set-point approach to homeostasis could have evolved (Weingarten, 1985). It would be an absolute impossibility for most mammals to survive if they ceased a particular behaviour once their immediate needs were met. Therefore, any explanation of motivated behaviours will need to include more than just reference to homeostatic needs and their fulfilment in order to explain even the fairly narrow range of behaviours which they attempt to cover.

• The theory takes little account of **cognitive processes**, which must be involved in the behavioural aspects of temperature regulation. If we are going to explain the prospective aspects of the theory there must be an incentive for that particular behaviour, although it is difficult to apply this criticism to animals as their temperature-regulating behaviour is almost entirely automatic or instinctive.

The shortcomings of this theory have led to the development of an alternative theory: **positive incentive theory.** This looks at the positive incentive value (Toates, 1981) of a particular behaviour and suggests that the incentive for such behaviours does not lie in the fulfilment of basic drives, but from the anticipated pleasure of future actions. In relation to temperature regulation, this might well equate to the process of bed warming on a cold night, even though when that behaviour is carried out there is no immediate biological drive being fulfilled.

This theory takes a number of different factors into account instead of just concentrating on one. In this way it can take account of the cognitive processes behind seemingly unnecessary or even undesirable behaviours like eating chocolate cake in spite of the fact that you may have just eaten a large meal.

Chapter summary

This chapter has identified **instinct/drive, incentive** and **arousal**, as possible motives for behaviour. The chapter has considered the influence of instincts and drives on behaviour, particularly concerning survival instincts; sex, eating, drinking and sleeping, as well as the drives behind temperature regulation. The CNS, ANS and endocrine

system have been reviewed in relation to their influence on physiological drives. The main features of homeostasis have been looked
at as part of an explanation of basic motivated behaviours and the
limitations of these have been discussed in relation to more complex
behaviours. These main features include a prospective element, as
well as the other biological processes of detection and control, which
helps us to predict future changes in the homeostatic balance and
prepare for them (carrying an umbrella before it starts raining).
A complementary alternative view to this has been put forward in the
shape of positive incentive theory.

Review exercise

Try to explain the following behaviours in terms of homeostatic factors and
provide an alternative explanation that doesn't rely on homeostatic control.
(A couple of examples are provided to start you off.)

	Homeostatic	Non-homeostatic
Eating	Energy maintenance	'That looks tasty'
Drinking		
Sleeping		
Temperature regulation		
Sex		

Further reading

Silber, K. (1999) *The Physiological Basis of Behaviour*. London:
Routledge. Part of this series of books and a very useful and direct
insight into the whole area of physiological influences.

Motivation and the brain: hunger

Hunger

The study of motivation based around physiological drives is particularly influential in the study of behaviour which satisfies physical drives such as eating and drinking. This chapter specifically considers the role of the brain in the identification, initiation and cessation of our drive to eat.

Some of the questions which need to be answered in relation to these processes include:

Why do we eat?
When do we eat?
What do we eat?
Why do some people eat more/less than others?

It may seem reasonably obvious why people eat (because they are hungry), but it is perhaps not so clear what it is that makes us feel hungry; what we feel hungry for; why we eat when we do, and what it is that makes us stop eating once we start.

It is not enough to simply claim that we eat because we are hungry or that we stop eating because we are 'full'. There are a variety of ways that our bodies respond to our need for food. In the same way as a car will respond to its needs in a variety of ways, so the body will respond to its need for food with more than just a rumble.

A car will show a number of signs that it is not getting enough petrol, it is not getting the right kind of oil or it is running low on other necessary fluids. Some of these signs will be obvious and easy to recognise (the car stops running), others will be subtler (such as rust). In relation to the human body, this might be equivalent to the obvious signs of lethargy, or the subtler appearance of white dots under our fingernails.

Progress exercise

Think about the signs that indicate you need to eat. Try to identify the various signals, which will be sent out by the body to suggest that you need food.

In order to understand our motivation for food we must first be able to recognise the signs that we are hungry and be able to identify where the motivation has arisen from.

How do we know we are hungry?

The identification of hunger will often involve a subjective experience of the 'feeling' of hunger, just as much as it will involve the objective/physical symptoms. Most people will feel hungry, even if they are not experiencing any significant physical effects. Most often these subjective feelings will involve a 'feeling' of emptiness or the feeling that it is time to eat.

This 'everyday' experience of hunger was first investigated by Monello and Mayer (1967). They gave out questionnaires, which asked about physical sensations and moods as well as thoughts of food. The kind of subjective feelings, mentioned above, were identified as important in this study, although people also reported sensations in the mouth, throat and head.

The connection between biological factors and the feeling of hunger centres around the role of the nervous system, in particular its role in maintaining a constant physical state at all times (homeostasis).

Homeostasis and hunger

The process of homeostasis has been outlined in the first chapter, but in relation to hunger the belief is that once the body falls below a set level of food/nutrients, mechanisms are triggered to motivate eating behaviour. The actual mechanisms involved in producing such behaviour have been the subject of much debate for many years and are still not completely understood.

One of the first mechanisms to be identified was by Cannon and Washburn (1912), who argued that the need for food was driven by the lack of food in the stomach. It was their belief that eating behaviour was motivated by the feeling of contractions (**hunger pangs**) in the stomach which sent messages to the brain (via the **vagus nerve**) to tell the body to start eating. This theory does at least fit in with the research of Monello and Mayer (mentioned earlier), in that we eat when we feel hungry, i.e. our stomach rumbles.

Do you only eat when you feel hungry?

What other factors might make you want to eat?

Progress exercise

Cannon and Washburn's rather simplistic explanation for the feeling of hunger has been subjected to much criticism following studies of cancer patients and '**sham-fed**' rats. The cancer patients were still able to regulate their food intake, in spite of having had their stomachs removed. The rats ate normal-sized meals even though their food was prevented from reaching their stomachs. In each of these cases the intake of food was maintained at normal levels in spite of the lack of messages from the stomach.

However, more recent studies (Leibowitz, 1992; Koopmans, 1981; Antin et al., 1978) have shown that either 'sham-fed' rats will over-eat (suggesting that the stomach is important in food regulation) or that other mechanisms apart from stomach rumbling are involved in the feeling of hunger, e.g. peptides. Peptides like **cholesystokinin** (CCK) are released as chemicals into the bloodstream, which provide the brain with information about hunger and **satiety**. They seem to operate in conjunction with the presence of food in the stomach to send messages to the brain via the vagus nerve. Such findings indicate support for the role of homeostasis in directing our eating behaviour, but also indicate that other factors may be responsible for controlling the actual messages sent.

Glucostatic theory

Mayer and Marshall (1956) have put forward a **glucostatic** version of the homeostasis theory. This proposes that we need to maintain our glucose (blood sugar) levels and therefore we are motivated to eat as these levels fall. They hypothesised a connection between glucose satiety and the hypothalamus. They suggested that there are glucose receptor cells in the brain (probably located in the lateral hypothalamus). The theory seems to be particularly strong, as glucose is the brain's primary source of energy.

More recent studies also provide support for this theory, in particular the work of Campfield and Smith (1990). In a typical Campfield and Smith experiment rats are provided with access to food and water, whilst their glucose levels are monitored. In this situation there is little change in the blood-sugar levels until 10 minutes before feeding time, at which point the levels suddenly drop by about 8 per cent.

This seems to suggest that the rat is responding to falling blood-sugar levels by taking on food to replenish them. But does it really?

Evaluation

- The apparent cause and effect relationship in this situation could, just as easily, be the opposite of what Campfield and Smith claim, i.e. that the decline in blood-sugar levels was the effect of the decision to eat rather than the cause of it. In this experiment the fall in blood sugar was itself preceded by a rise in **insulin** levels. The animals appeared to lower their own blood-sugar levels by releasing insulin, thus making them ready to start eating. This conclusion is supported by the fact that the fall in blood sugar occurred dramatically, shortly before eating, rather than gradually as one might expect if this theory were true.
- Other experiments with food-deprived animals (Russek, 1971) have suggested that the liver may be the site for monitoring glucose levels. Russek showed that injections of glucose will prevent eating in animals if it is injected into the liver, but not if it is injected in any other area. If this is true then cellular glucose rather than blood glucose is the deciding factor in hunger.
- Furthermore, if the blood-glucose version of this theory were true then surely the only things we would eat would be foods that contribute to raising this level. This may well explain our desire to eat sweet foods, but it doesn't explain our desire for foods which contribute nothing to glucose levels e.g. fats.
- It may be useful to see the need to maintain glucose as a very important factor in eating (no doubt many people have felt the effects of low glucose levels in the form of tiredness and head-aches), but like the need for the presence of food in the stomach, it is certainly not the only one.
- These explanations fail to take into account the influence of environmental factors, which can have a very strong influence on our eating behaviour. When we visit a supermarket or restaurant we are bombarded by the sight and smell of food, which in itself can cause us to feel hungry, even when we have recently eaten. This feeling would of course be strengthened if we hadn't eaten, hence the belief that you should never go shopping on an empty stomach, as you always spend too much money.

Whilst visiting the supermarket or going to a restaurant may only be applicable to human behaviour, the influence of the environment is just as important in the study of animal behaviour. It is possible to see food-seeking behaviour as purely goal-directed, but an animal's tendency to express this behaviour will fluctuate depending on its internal state. Animals that have recently eaten will ignore the same food that would have been sought when they were hungry. Therefore, it is necessary to see food-seeking behaviour as part of a whole system, which involves the organism and its environment (Toates, 1986).

The influence of environmental factors and the specific mechanisms involved in deciding what, when and how much to eat will be considered next when we look at the regulation of eating and body weight.

Why don't we eat ourselves to death?

In more primitive times the decision to eat would have been decided by the availability of food. As society has progressed and food has become more readily available there have been problems with **obesity** e.g. 4/10 of Americans are officially obese. In spite of this, and the growing problem of obesity in the West, we still need to understand why it is that most people are able to maintain a stable body weight.

There are two main aspects to this:

- The regulation of food intake.
- The regulation of body weight.

Most people, most of the time, eat in a fairly uniform regular way. The question is, how much of this is controlled by physiological factors, and how much is controlled by other factors, e.g. time of day?

Support for the physiological/homeostatic explanation of food intake has already been discussed above, but is further supported by Davis's (1928) famous cafeteria study. Children were presented with a selection of foods and allowed to choose what to eat at meal times. According to Davis, they *chose* to eat a balanced diet. However, no strongly sweet foods were provided and further studies have shown that children and animals will over-eat sugary foods if they are available. Children will also eat more Smarties if they are multi-coloured than if they are all of one colour (Rolls, Rowe and

Rolls, 1982). This suggests that regulation of food intake is far more complicated than just the homeostatic needs of each individual.

Consider the factors of the *sight, taste* and *smell* of food.

Suggest how these three might be influenced by:

- Individual differences
- Cultural differences

Progress exercise

There is no doubt that the *sight, taste* and *smell* of food will influence what we eat, but the differences between individuals and cultures suggested above brings the influence of physiological factors into question. What we eat, when we eat and even how much we eat are as much influenced by these individual and cultural differences as much as they are by biological needs.

Whilst this section cannot provide a definitive answer to the question of why we don't eat ourselves to death, it will look at a number of important environmental and physiological explanations, including the role of the hypothalamus.

The role of the hypothalamus

The hypothalamus is a small but very important part of the brain. It forms part of the posterior forebrain and is located just below the anterior **thalamus** ('hypo' means below). The importance of this area can be seen from the number of neural tracts entering and leaving it, connecting it to a number of other areas within the central nervous system (CNS). It is particularly important in our understanding of motivated behaviours and is seen to exert its influence through regulation of the pituitary gland.

Evidence to support the role of the hypothalamus in controlling eating behaviour comes from the study of rats. There are some suggestions that damage to one of two sections of the hypothalamus can cause over-eating (**hyperphagia**) or the cessation of eating (**aphagia**) in rats.

It has long been believed that these two sections work in tandem to control our eating behaviour. This is known as the **dual hypothalamic control** theory of eating. The theory suggests that the **lateral hypothalamus (LH)** serves to 'turn on' the desire for food, whilst the **ventromedial hypothalamus (VMH)** turns it off.

How could this theory be tested?

What problems might arise from our desire to test this theory?

The implications of this theory for testing should be reasonably clear and reasonably controversial. If you want to test it, you must destroy the capability of one of these sections and observe the effect. If this theory is correct then damage (**lesions**) to the LH should cause aphagia, damage to the VMH should cause hyperphagia.

Ventromedial hypothalamus

Early research into this area seemed to provide reasonably conclusive evidence. Hetherington and Ranson (1940) tested the effect of VMH lesions on rats. They showed that VMH-lesioned rats over-eat and become extremely obese, leading to a tripling of normal body weight in some. This VMH syndrome consisted of two distinct phases:

- The dynamic phase – the rat gains weight dramatically over the course of a few weeks of grossly excessive eating.
- The static phase – following weeks of this excessive behaviour, consumption gradually declines until the rat is eating only enough to maintain its level of obesity.

This stable level will hereafter be maintained in spite of the amount of food available. If the amount is decreased for a while, the rat will increase its intake later in order to return to its obese level. If the rat is force fed for a time, it will decrease later intake to achieve the same result. This effect can be seen in human behaviour also. There will have been times when most people will have had to go without food for longer than usual. This period is generally followed by a period of 'extra' eating to try and make up for the food that has been 'missed'.

An alternative view of the role of the VMH in eating comes from the **cephalic phase hypothesis** (Powley, 1977). He suggests that lesions to the VMH affect the palatability of food, such that normally palatable food tastes better and normally unpalatable food tastes worse. Therefore, the amount of food consumed is altered as a result of the change in palatability. The VMH lesions lead to exaggerated autonomic and endocrine responses in the rats to the smell and taste of food (Powley refers to these responses as cephalic reflexes of digestion). These responses are most likely to be an exaggerated increase in saliva or insulin, causing the rat to want to eat more than is necessary.

The difference here is that it is not over-eating that causes the rat to gain weight but a change in its metabolic activity in response to the presence of food. This change leads to a speeding up in the process of **lipogenesis** (the conversion of nutrients into body fat), which in turn means the rat must eat more to ensure it has enough calories in its blood to maintain energy levels.

In order to prevent over-eating then, the connection between the brain and the pancreas would need to be cut in order to prevent the increased production of insulin. This has been tested by cutting the vagus nerve (discussed earlier) leading to a decrease in VMH rats' eating (Cox and Powley, 1981).

Further support for the role of the VMH in satiety comes from research which showed that **electrical stimulation** of the VMH in rats will prevent eating until the stimulation stops. Although this evidence may seem conclusive at first sight, it suffers from a number of problems (discussed below), but one issue is immediately problematic.

If the VMH controls eating, why don't the rats continue eating until they died? Why do they stop?

If the role of the VMH can be questioned due to this tendency for the effects to wear off, the same cannot be said of research into the role of the lateral hypothalamus (LH).

Lateral hypothalamus

Anand and Brobeck (1951) produced lesions in the LH, which caused aphagia; these rats literally starved themselves to death. As with the VMH rats it was found that electrical stimulation of the LH had an effect, in this case it caused the rat to start eating. However, the extent to which this evidence is more conclusive than the VMH research must be questioned by the fact that death from stopping eating will come more quickly than from over-eating. This is particularly significant when the fact that LH lesions also caused **adipsia** (a complete cessation of drinking), is taken into account (Teitelbaum and Epstein, 1962).

Evaluation of dual hypothalamic control

- Apart from the problem with the static phase of VMH syndrome mentioned earlier, the role of the VMH can be questioned by the findings of Teitelbaum (1955) who showed that VMH rats are less likely to eat unpalatable food than normally hungry rats and are less likely to eat if they have to work for the food.
- A similar effect is shown by an experiment conducted by Schachter (1971), which found that obese (human) participants were less likely to eat unshelled nuts but more likely to eat shelled ones.
- However, other research has shown that 'fussiness' in eating is a consequence of obesity itself, not of VMH lesions. Weingarten, Chang and Jarvie (1983) found that VMH rats are no less likely to eat unpalatable food than are non-VMH rats of similar obesity.
- A more radical explanation of the increasing body weight of VMH rats has come from Booth (1994), who suggests that VMH lesions cause the stomach to empty abnormally quickly requiring the extra ingestion of food. But also, that insulin levels increase, causing more of the food to be turned to fat, so the VMH rats become fatter, whether they eat more food or not.
- The role of the LH in eating has been questioned by the finding that the effects of LH lesions are reversible (Teitelbaum and Epstein, 1962). Rats were able to recover their desire for food as long as they were kept alive through the initial phase by being tube fed. In a similar way to the VMH rats they showed virtually normal eating patterns after a few weeks.

- Other findings of research with LH rats have shown that they suffer from behavioural disturbances that are not connected to eating (poor balance and a lack of response to any sensory stimuli). It has also been found that electrical stimulation of other areas of the brain produces similar findings to LH stimulation i.e. rats eat more. In light of such evidence the idea that the LH can be identified as a discrete feeding centre, which alone controls the desire for food, must be re-assessed.
- However, Rolls and Rolls (1982) have found that neurons in the LH do respond to palatable foods, at least when they are originally presented, but these responses decline if the food is presented often. This suggests that the LH does play some role in our responsiveness to food and is activated in response to new and exciting foods, suggesting that in a natural state it does play an important part in our desire to search for food and in the regulation of body weight.

In a review of the origins of ingestive behaviour, Stricker (1990) suggests that LH lesions do not destroy the body's feeding centre, but instead affect some non-specific aspect of arousal in the motivation for feeding, which will (if given time) be adapted to by the rats in the ways outlined above.

> There is a more general problem with all of the studies looked at so far. Read back through the previous section and identify a point of evaluation that is applicable to (nearly) all of them.

Progress exercise

Lipostatic theory

The role of the hypothalamus is seen to be particularly important in the maintenance of a stable level of body fat.

According to **lipostatic theory**, body weight is regulated by a body-fat set point. Our bodies store fats or **lipids** in specialised cells called **adipocytes**. When fat deposits fall below a person's set point, they must eat in order to restore the required level of fat. Changes in the amount of fat stored have a significant effect on body weight and it seems likely therefore that fat **metabolism** is an important aspect of food-intake decisions and body-weight regulation.

The main proponent of this theory, Nisbett (1972), suggests (as above) that our bodies have a body-weight set point, which is maintained within fairly narrow limits, so that each individual's weight will change very little. The levels of fat stored in the adipocytes determine this set point and the number of adipocytes is determined in childhood by our eating behaviour. During normal metabolic activity these levels fall. Once they fall below the required level (set point), messages are sent through the nervous system to the hypothalamus to start eating.

As we have already seen, damage to the hypothalamus can affect our ability to recognise these messages and can lead to over-eating or under-eating depending on the region in which the damage occurs. In relation to lipostatic theory, lesions to the VMH may have caused the set point to be artificially raised causing the rats to eat more food in order to reach the new target, as this target was too high they over-ate and became obese.

Progress exercise

What other possible explanations can you think of to explain the rats' eating behaviour?

Evaluation

- This theory is completely plausible as long as we accept that the desire to reach the set point was the only factor involved in the rats' eating behaviour.
- However, evidence from VMH rats has also shown that lesions increase blood insulin levels, which in turn causes an increase in

lipogenesis (the production of body fat) and brings about a decrease in **lipolysis** (the breakdown of body fat into energy), (Powley et al., 1980). It seems then that the rats are responding to the need to maintain energy levels rather than the need to maintain a set point. The calories of the rats were converted into fat at a very high rate, which meant that the rats needed to eat more to simply provide enough calories to give them their required levels of energy, providing further support for the glucostatic theory discussed earlier.

- Although there is little strong empirical evidence for this theory, an experiment with LH-lesioned rats by Keesey and Powley (1975) has provided some support. They lowered the weight of the rats prior to the lesion and found that rather than the lesion causing *aphagia* (as above); the rats actually ate more.

- One possible explanation for this is that damage to the hypothalamus does not have a direct effect on eating behaviour, but does have an indirect effect by altering the animals body-fat/weight set point. In the case quoted above the rats' eating behaviour has been artificially disturbed prior to the lesion, so even though the lesion may have lowered the set point, it was still above the weight that had been achieved prior to the lesion, so the rats ate more.

- This theory is useful in understanding the stability of body weight and fat and to some extent in showing how differences in the number of fat cells will cause individual differences in weight and fat levels. If we all have a set point that is determined in childhood, then our body weight and fat levels in later life will be maintained around this set point, which will be different for all individuals depending on their eating behaviour during childhood. Therefore, if you are fat there's nothing you can do about it except perhaps blame your parents for not feeding you right when you were a child.

Settling-point hypothesis

However, there are further problems for this theory when we examine the success or otherwise of weight-loss programmes. Anyone who has ever tried to lose weight will know the disappointment experienced after the first few weeks of weight loss, when it becomes increasingly difficult to lose any more weight. Part of the answer to this may come from a rejection of the set-point view in favour of a **settling-point hypothesis**. According to this view, body weight is not determined by set levels that must be achieved for normal functioning, rather it fluctuates around a level at which various factors interact to achieve a balance or equilibrium (Pinel, 1997).

Changes in food intake and body fat are modified in this view by further changes in the homeostatic regulatory system in order to bring about this balance. Although the initial changes will bring about rapid weight loss, the system's response to this will bring about other changes that will serve to limit the amount of weight loss.

In many ways of course, this doesn't seem particularly different to the set-point view, both suggest that homeostatic changes will occur in response to weight loss or gain in order to bring the body back to what it was before. An important distinction, particularly for anyone trying to lose weight is that the set-point view regards these changes as irrepressible, whereas the settling-point hypothesis suggests that they only have an effect if the behaviour that brought about the weight loss/gain is terminated or isn't enhanced by some other change in behaviour. Therefore, although your body will fight against your attempts to lose weight, it can be achieved by a permanent change in one or more of the factors that influence the settling point (fat content of food, exercise, etc.).

So, just in case anyone needs reminding CRASH DIETING DOESN'T WORK. At least not in the long run anyway.

Obesity

One analysis of human obesity comes from a summary of research by Schachter (1971), which suggests that there are many similarities between the behaviour of VMH-lesioned rats and obese humans. The main similarity with VMH rats is that like the VMH rats, the obese are governed by external factors in their eating behaviour. External factors such as time of day, taste of food and the amount of effort required govern the eating behaviour of obese humans, whereas internal factors such as homeostatic cues govern the eating behaviour of non-obese humans. Schachter conducted a range of studies comparing non-obese people with obese people, which appeared to show that obese people would eat more when a clock is artificially speeded up and were less likely to eat food that had been made unpalatable.

However, Rodin (1981) reviewed a range of research herself and found that many studies have been unable to identify any link between obesity and external cues. She suggests that external cues affect obese and non-obese people and many obese people show no responsiveness to external cues.

An alternative view to this comes from Nisbett (1972) who suggested a more influential role for the idea of a body-weight set point. According to this view, there is no behavioural difference between obese and non-obese subjects who are at or close to their individual body-weight set point. In a study involving eating ice cream, Nisbett (1968) found that the behaviour of obese people who had lost weight was similar to underweight people and that if any individual in any of the weight groups fell below their set point, their eating behaviour was more like that associated with the obese.

So why do some people have body-weight set points that are higher than others? Stricker (1978) argues that there are two types of obesity:

1. This occurs in response to non-hunger-related factors such as the availability of good-tasting food, increased arousal and stress.
2. This occurs due to individual metabolic differences. Such differences involve body fuels being driven out into the blood and depositing themselves in fat cells (formed in childhood perhaps), which leaves other cells starved of fuel, thus promoting further desires for food.

All of this seems to suggest that whilst type 1 people may be able to overcome their obesity once these factors change or are removed, type 2 people are fighting a losing battle. It seems that, due to these individual differences, some people will have a constant struggle against obesity, whilst others will be able to maintain a low body weight with no effort at all. It also suggests that such people will never be able to maintain a lower body weight for any length of time, as they will always return to their set point.

It may also be that obesity has more to do with **genetics** and our evolutionary past. Humans have evolved in a situation requiring the need for competition over sometimes scarce and always unreliable food sources, in this situation the storage of fat for energy can be seen as adaptive. In the past this storage would have been regulated by famine rather than by choice and therefore the ability to regulate eating behaviour in situations where food is abundant (the West) is not present in the genetic make up of at least some individuals.

This may help to explain the 'perceived' increasing problem of obesity in countries like Britain and America and may also suggest that the growing market for weight-loss products and programmes may all be a waste of time and may in fact be purely driven by a desire to achieve a body image that is culturally specific, rather than physically necessary.

Anorexia nervosa

An individual who fails to eat enough food to satisfy their physical needs even when such food is readily available is said to be suffering from the eating disorder **anorexia nervosa**. Bruch (1973) describes it as 'the relentless pursuit of thinness through self-starvation, even unto death'.

Although some of the evidence above (LH lesions causing aphagia in rats) may be regarded as informative in relation to this problem, it is certainly less plausible as a real *explanation*.

Whilst it is plausible to assume that similar genetic influences or **socialisation** may cause some individuals to achieve a very low weight/fat level, the fact that the condition affects around 1 per cent of females in the 12-to-18 age group and that only 5 per cent of anorexics are male suggests that other explanations must be sought.

Typical symptoms of anorexia include:

- A reduction of at least 25 per cent of original body weight.
- A distorted view of body size, such that they believe they are fat when they are clearly underweight.
- The absence of menstruation.

The most often cited social-psychological explanation concerns the Western image of the ideal woman, which is presented through the media. Coupled with the increasing pressure on adolescents to 'fit in' and for teenage girls to find romance, this image can have a powerful effect.

In psychological terms, this explanation would combine with the establishment of an **ideal self-image** during socialisation. If this self-image conflicts with normal eating behaviour then problems are bound to arise.

A further psychological approach suggests that it may be used by the sufferer as a way of gaining attention from parents or as a way of gaining control from domineering or over-demanding parents.

There also appear to be physiological factors associated with anorexia and the absence of menstruation. Some (Garfinkel and Garner, 1982) have suggested that a disturbance in the hypothalamus may well be the cause of anorexia, as this plays an important role in hormonal functions, which would also affect menstruation. However, although there is some evidence for such differences between anorexics and non-anorexics, it is not clear whether the disturbance caused the anorexia or the anorexia caused the disturbance.

This evidence suggests that there are psychological motives for this behaviour, which are at best not yet understood and at worst symptomatic of a severe form of mental disorder (further explanations of this problem can be found in the book on psychopathologies in this series).

What is more clear though is that anorexia is an increasing problem, Logue (1991) found that the actual occurrence, not just reported occurrence of anorexia had increased during the previous 25 to 35 years.

All of this suggests that what is currently regarded as 'normal' weight will soon be very far from the average weight.

Chapter summary

In this chapter we have looked at the relationship between motivated behaviour and physiology. Specifically, the connection between brain mechanisms/activity and the identification of hunger.

Homeostatic mechanisms have been considered in the identification of hunger, which suggest that there are pre-set levels which must be maintained in order to keep the body in a state of balance. One such pre-set level is glucose, which according to glucostatic theory, is maintained by the initiation of eating behaviour as the set level falls. However, critics of the homeostatic view believe that such set levels are only a part of the process, which should be considered alongside social, environmental and cultural factors.

The role of the hypothalamus has been discussed in relation to the regulation of food intake. The dual hypothalamic control theory of eating suggests that the lateral hypothalamus turns on the desire for food, whilst the ventromedial hypothalamus turns it off. Research involving lesions to these regions of rats' brains has provided support for this view, causing the rats to over- or under-eat. However, there has been little research with humans (for obvious reasons), and research that has been conducted suggests other factors are involved.

Lipostatic theory has been considered as an explanation for the regulation of body weight, suggesting a body-fat set point (established during childhood) which is maintained homeostatically. The idea of a set point has been opposed by the settling-point hypothesis, suggesting that changes in eating behaviour cause the body to achieve a new state of balance at a different level of body weight than before, as long as the changes are permanent.

Important practical applications of these theories have been identified in relation to obesity and anorexia nervosa, although a more detailed psychological analysis of both of these would be necessary for a fuller (but still incomplete) answer.

Review exercise

Numbered below are each of the main headings/concepts contained in this chapter.

See if you can match them up with the lettered explanations provided below them.

1 Glucostatic theory
2 Homeostasis
3 Regulation of food intake
4 Obesity
5 Lipostatic theory
6 Regulation of body weight
7 The hypothalamus
8 Anorexia

continued . . .

MOTIVATION AND THE BRAIN: HUNGER

A The part of the brain that is believed to contain discrete feeding centres.

B An eating disorder characterised by a mistaken perception of being overweight.

C Hunger being identified by blood-glucose levels.

D The control of the type and amount of food eaten.

E The mechanism responsible for maintaining a stable state within our bodies.

F A condition caused by excessive over-eating.

G Maintaining your weight within set limits.

H The body has set levels of fat that determine how much we eat.

For each of the numbered concepts provide an example/statement that helps explain the concept further. When you have finished go back to the text and check whether or not you were correct.

Further reading

Pinel, John P.J. (1997) *Biopsychology*. 3rd edn. Boston, MA: Allyn & Bacon. Chapter 10. This is an excellent text, covering a wide area of biopsychology topics. Some of the material is quite advanced, but this chapter is written in an amusing and accessible style, with some useful illustrations.

Wong, R. (2000) *Motivation: a biobehavioural approach*. Cambridge: Cambridge University Press. Chapters 4 and 5 offer a more detailed analysis of the hunger issues explored in this chapter.

4

Motivation and the brain: thirst

Thirst and drinking
How do we know we are thirsty?
Types of thirst
What makes us stop drinking?
Alcohol and alcoholism
Chapter summary

Thirst and drinking

How many times have you said or heard others say: 'I really need a drink'? But how often was that really true? Was a drink really needed, or was it that the pleasurable effect of a particular flavour or substance was required?

In order to answer such questions, we must first pose a few more:

What is it that makes us drink?
What do we get thirsty for?
Are there specific events that make us thirsty?
How much do we need to drink?

A complete answer to all of these questions is probably not possible (particularly the last one), but this section will show the connection between these issues and specific physiological mechanisms.

How do we know we are thirsty?

As with the previous chapter on hunger the answer to this may seem obvious at first, but perhaps less so when we think about it for a little longer. There are similar physiological, environmental *and* cognitive processes at work in relation to thirst, as there are with hunger, which will all play a part in answering this question.

It would be useful at this point to try to identify the signs that you are thirsty, as you have already done with hunger in the previous chapter.

Perhaps the most obvious sign is a dry mouth, throat or lips. But if these were the only ways of recognising that we wanted a drink then we would only drink when these signs occurred. Obviously, we do not and therefore there must be other factors involved.

To return to the car analogy put forward in the previous chapter on hunger, it would not be a good idea to wait until your car ran dry of the fluids necessary for its efficient functioning before adding more. Efficient maintenance of a car requires such fluids to be topped up on a regular basis, otherwise the engine will seize up and the whole system ceases to function at all.

In relation to the human body, it would similarly not be a good idea to run your fluids down until you are near the mark of not functioning.

Our bodies will (as mentioned in Chapter 3) try to maintain a stable state, this tendency is called homeostasis.

Homeostasis and fluid regulation

Our bodies need to maintain a regular amount of water for a number of reasons, but it is perhaps simplest to say that certain physical processes, e.g. blood circulation, rely on the maintenance of a constant level of water for their normal functioning.

Bodily processes such as breathing, sweating and urination all involve water loss, but some of them also involve the loss of other substances, such as sodium.

Not only do our bodies need to regulate the amount of water outside cells (**extracellular**); they also need to regulate the concentration of water and electrolytes within cells (**intracellular**). Body cells die if intracellular water is reduced beyond a certain level.

In relation to water, the body can be thought of as a container for two separate fluid-filled compartments: the intracellular compartment, which holds about two-thirds of the body's water; and the extracellular compartment, which holds the other third and is contained within the blood, the **interstitial fluid** and the **cerebrospinal fluid**.

The fluid in the intracellular compartment is separated from the interstitial fluid (the fluid which surrounds all cells) by membranes, which prevent the flow of certain substances, such as sodium, but allow the flow of water.

Normally the fluids in both compartments can be described as **isotonic,** that is they contain equal concentrations of solutes (dissolved substances), the most important of which is sodium chloride (common table salt). If the concentration of a solute rises, the fluid becomes **hypertonic** and will need to draw more water into it. If the concentration falls, it becomes **hypotonic** and will need to release water. Consequently, these two compartments are involved in a constant process of passing water from one to the other; this process is called **osmosis**.

These factors should help in an appreciation of the types of thirst that we all encounter on a daily basis. Thirst will therefore be caused by either:

1. The loss of water *volume* in the extracellular compartment, e.g. through bleeding (volumetric thirst).
2. Cellular dehydration in the intracellular compartment, caused by an imbalance in the extracellular compartment, requiring water to be drawn from the cells, e.g. due to sweating or urination (osmotic thirst).

Types of thirst

Osmotic thirst

The information provided so far should give you a better understanding as to why fast-food joints smother their fries in salt and why pubs sell salted snacks (some even provide them free).

From their point of view it is good business to encourage you to purchase more drinks by stimulating cellular dehydration in your body. The more salt that goes in, the more water is needed to promote an isotonic solution; the more you drink.

This type of thirst is called **osmotic thirst.**

Osmotic pressure is built up in the way suggested above due to the creation of a hypertonic solution outside the cells, caused by the normal daily loss of water through urination, sweating and even breathing. This process is further complicated by the intake of solutes from eating, thus leading to the need to draw water from inside the cells. In order to bring back a balance we must take in more water, so that the extracellular compartment has the same concentration as the intracellular compartment.

This process occurs very quickly, suggesting that the receptors for this information are most likely to be in the brain.

Osmoreceptors

There are two sets of **osmoreceptors**, which have been identified as important in responding to **osmotic pressure**.

The first set have been identified in both the lateral preoptic (LPO) region of the hypothalamus (Peck and Blass, 1975), and the lateral hypothalamus (Oomura et al., 1969). These promote drinking behaviour when they are stimulated, and appear to respond directly to levels of salt in the body.

Peck and Blass (1975) using micro-injections of a hypertonic solution, found that when salt was injected into the **preoptic nucleus** of the hypothalamus, drinking behaviour followed. When it was injected elsewhere, it did not.

The second set of receptors have been identified in an area of the hypothalamus called the *nucleus circularis* (Hatton, 1976), who found that electrical stimulation of this area led to water retention. This second set of receptors promote water retention in the kidneys by releasing a hormone from the pituitary gland. When this **antidiuretic hormone (ADH)** is released into the blood it causes the kidneys to retain water, but not salt. As the kidneys control the amount of salt and water we excrete through the production of urine, the effect is that the urine produced is particularly concentrated with salt (more yellow). This is particularly useful, as it may not always be possible to initiate drinking behaviour immediately.

All of this suggests that the process of recognising that we are thirsty and the mechanisms that make us stop and start are fairly simple and uncomplicated. As we shall see below, this is very far from true and particular problems arise when we look at the role of the mouth in this process.

Think about times when you have been particularly thirsty (presumably those osmoreceptors were telling you to have a drink), was it always necessary to consume significant amounts of liquid? It may have been enough to simply wet your lips (at least in the short term). Try this for yourself next time you feel really thirsty. Why do you think it helps? Is it purely due to physical factors, or are psychological factors coming into play?

Progress exercise

Volumetric thirst

Loss of water volume from the extracellular compartment most commonly occurs due to a sudden and large-scale loss of blood; the part of our blood that is not made up of red or white blood cells (plasma) is mostly water. As with osmotic thirst the receptors for **volumetric thirst** need to be able to start working quickly or the blood loss will stop the heart functioning properly.

Obviously at those times when blood is lost, it is not always possible to start drinking so these receptors need to have other water-retaining effects as well. There are two types of receptor responsible for this type of thirst.

The first are **baroreceptors** in the heart, which send messages to the **median preoptic nucleus** of the hypothalamus and promote the production of ADH. Research with rats has shown that the injection of colloids (substances that draw plasma from the blood) into kidney-less rats causes them to drink (Stricker, 1972).

The second group of receptors are in the kidneys, these are blood-flow receptors and as their name suggests they respond to changes in blood flow, as well as the newly produced ADH. They stimulate the production of a hormone renin, which causes the formation of the hormone **angiotensin II.** This has a number of effects:

1. It causes blood vessels to constrict, increasing blood pressure.
2. It triggers the release of aldosterone, causing the kidneys to re-absorb salt. This is important because high concentrations of salt in the blood will lead to more water being retained.
3. It seems to be able to reach another part of the brain, the **subfornical organ**, which stimulates drinking behaviour.

These two sets of receptors will help us maintain water volume by both direct acts of drinking behaviour and by encouraging the retention of the water that is already present. As such they appear to be suitable mechanisms to deal with problems that are caused by blood loss.

Progress exercise

Look back through the two previous sections concerning the two types of thirst. Provide a summary of the processes involved in the two types by completing the following sentences for each one.

Osmotic/volumetric thirst is caused by . . .
A lack of water is identified by . . .
These receptors stimulate water retention/drinking behaviour by . . .

Evaluation

- Evidence for the processes involved in osmotic and volumetric thirst has been put forward, but the precise mechanisms are complex and unclear.
- However, as early as 1962 Fisher and Coury were able to demonstrate successfully how the injection of drugs that increase the activity of the **neurotransmitter** called **acetylcholine** into

various regions of the brain produced drinking behaviour in non-thirsty rats.

- Evidence from Fitzsimmons and Moore-Gillon (1980) has shown that reducing the amount of blood reaching the heart results in drinking, and artificially stimulating the baroreceptors results in reduced drinking, suggesting that the baroreceptors in the heart are particularly important for the recognition of thirst.
- Further work by Fitzsimmons has also shown that these results occur in spite of the amount of angiotensin in the system, showing that both sets of receptors are working independently of one another.
- Fitzsimmons and Simons (1969) also found that increasing the amount of angiotensin can bring about increased drinking without influencing other motivated behaviours, suggesting that, in relation to motivation, this is the sole purpose of this hormone.
- Whilst it is possible to consider the effects of intracellular and extracellular dehydration separately, it may be more useful to consider them together, as this is the way dehydration is likely to occur naturally.
- Rolls, Rolls and Wood (1980) looked at the effect of injecting rats that had been deprived of water overnight, with either water or a saline solution. They found that both had the effect of reducing drinking behaviour, suggesting that water deficits in each compartment converge in the lateral hypothalamus area of the brain to produce drinking behaviour and restore the appropriate balance.

Although the evidence presented above suggests that we need to maintain a constant level of fluid in the body, it does not exactly show how this occurs.

What makes us stop drinking?

As we saw in the first chapter, set-point theories believe that this behaviour will cease once the set point has been returned to.

However, this view suffers from similar criticisms to the set-point theory related to eating:

- Drinking stops before the fluid has had a chance to be absorbed fully.

- Animals (and humans) will drink more than they need when fluid is readily available.
- There are many cases of drinking where water deficits are not involved and therefore set-point theory could nether explain this nor what it is that stops it.

The first of these points has been tested in relation to the role of the presence of water in the mouth and there is some evidence to suggest that simply wetting the mouth has an effect on the drinking behaviour of thirsty rats (Wagner, 1999).

Similarly, experiments involving **sham drinking** in rats has shown that they will drink an amount equal to the amount required even though the liquid going into the rat's mouth is prevented from reaching the stomach by a tube inserted into a hole cut in the throat of the rat (Blass and Hall, 1976).

Furthermore, when similarly deprived rats have water injected directly into their stomach they are less likely to stop drinking than when water passes through the mouth (Rowland and Nicolaidis, 1976).

In these cases the mere presence of water in the mouth was enough to convince the rats that they were hydrated, suggesting that the mouth plays a very important role in the determination of how much we drink and is capable of determining how much we need to drink.

The second point cannot be dealt with so easily, as the evidence suggests that rats will continue drinking regardless of their level of thirst, if the fluid they have available to them has a pleasant taste.

Rolls, Wood and Stevens (1978) found that drinking behaviour in rats rose massively when small quantities of saccharin were added to their water. When the water is made unpalatable Engell and Hirsch (1991) found that people would not drink the amount they need to fully rehydrate.

However, when we are really thirsty we usually require drinks that have as little added to them as possible. After a long period of water deprivation or physical activity, the only drink that will really do is water.

In relation to the related aspect that we drink more than we need, Dicker and Nunn (1957) found that rats would reduce the level and frequency of urine excretion when less fluid was available to them and were still able to maintain a healthy state.

The evidence above shows that the pleasing taste of a drink or the mere fact that a drink is readily available will cause us to drink, suggesting that it is possible to drink a lot less than we do without any damaging effects to our health. Our bodies can quickly and easily learn to cope with the change.

The final point relates to what is known as **spontaneous drinking**. This is the drinking behaviour that occurs for most people most of the time, as most of us do not wait until we are dehydrated before commencing drinking.

This relates to the prospective element of homeostasis that was discussed in the first chapter. In short, we drink prospectively (before we get thirsty) in order to avoid future feelings of thirst, particularly when we know that we won't be able to have a drink for some time.

Primary and secondary drinking

The drinking behaviour that accompanies dehydration can be referred to as primary drinking as it satisfies a tangible physiological need. However, this internal factor is not the only thing that influences our drinking behaviour.

Any drinking that is not aimed towards dealing with internal needs can be regarded as secondary drinking. But as we have already seen we will sometimes drink in the absence of need to avoid later dehydration, so it may be better to regard secondary drinking as any behaviour that has no physiological basis, be it immediate or otherwise.

There are a number of external factors that can cause secondary drinking. Try to identify as many as possible in relation to the headings provided below, as well as any others you can think of yourself. (One is given to help you.)

Sight – advertisements for drink can make you feel thirsty.
Taste
Accessibility
Presence of others
Location
Time of day/year

Progress exercise

There are a number of external factors that influence drinking behaviour that have nothing to do with the physiological need for fluid or solutes. We will drink to be sociable, for the taste, due to the drink's visual appeal, because it has a pleasant taste or just because we are in a place that sells drinks, e.g. a pub.

Research has shown that drinking is motivated by the *positive incentive properties* of the drink (Rolls et al., 1980). We are therefore motivated to drink simply because we like the taste (fruit juice, milk etc.), but we may also be motivated by the pleasurable effects of certain drinks (alcohol, coffee etc.).

Booth (1991) has suggested that certain drinks have an optimal temperature, at which they will be at their most enjoyable and further that this temperature will be different in different countries e.g. beer has a different optimal temperature in Britain and America. In fact very few other countries in the world could tolerate the British love of warm beer. Added to this are factors to do with the time of day that it is deemed to be appropriate to consume certain drinks and that we are more likely to drink different types of drinks in the summer and winter.

Thus you can see that although we do have physiological needs that require satisfaction, our drinking behaviour is determined more by habit, culture and learning rather than any other internal or external factors.

Bolles (1979) suggests that experiments used to study the drinking behaviour of rats are far too simple to be relevant. According to Bolles the 'real rat' drinks for a variety of reasons, not just because it is thirsty. One of the main reasons appears to be a connection with food, in particular the rat drinks more when it is hungry and eats less when it is thirsty. A series of experiments by Falk (1961, 1972, 1977) lead him to the view that drinking and in particular polydypsia (over-drinking) can occur as a form of displacement activity in response to a frustrating situation. In his experiments rats were under-fed according to a schedule, which in turn caused them to drink more than three times their normal fluid intake (Falk, 1961).

The 'real rat' and perhaps the 'real human' respond to a variety of stimuli in their drinking behaviour and not just to satisfy homeostatic needs.

Alcohol and alcoholism

Alcohol is a drug that about two-thirds of the UK population regularly use and it is also a drug to which about one in ten of that two-thirds are addicted. Furthermore, alcohol is involved in about 40,000 deaths in the UK each year, from birth defects; alcohol related illnesses, accidents and violence.

Alcohol is such a problem because it attacks virtually every part of the body, causing brain damage in extreme cases (**Korsakoff's syndrome**), heart attacks, cirrhosis (scarring) of the liver and many other illnesses and damage.

It is for these reasons that many health and psychological professionals regard alcohol as a much more significant problem than any illegal drug. However, what is of interest here are the motivational properties of alcohol for all of us and for alcoholics in particular. Contrary to popular belief, alcohol is not a **stimulant**; it is in fact a **depressant**, causing those who take in moderate to high doses to lose control of cognitive and motor skills and at very high doses, leads to unconsciousness. Whilst at low levels it does stimulate neural activity and cause a pleasant feeling and a loss of inhibition, at higher levels it suppresses neural activity and causes a feeling of passivity and listlessness.

As with all drugs, alcohol disturbs the normal chemical balance of the body as it stimulates the activity of the inhibitory neurotransmitter GABA. It is this that leads to the depressant effect and according to the **physical dependence theory of addiction** is this that causes the dependence.

In order to understand the motivation for the continued use and abuse of alcohol, it is necessary to look at the issues of **tolerance, dependence and withdrawal.**

Continued use of alcohol in certain situations produces a tolerance to its effects, such that increasingly high doses need to be taken to produce the same effects. One of the tolerance effects of alcohol is that in heavy drinkers the liver metabolises alcohol at a much faster rate than casual drinkers, lessening the overall effect. Dependence on any drug arises from the physical and (often) psychological need to experience its effects, which is in turn linked to the withdrawal effects of not taking the drug. Therefore, it is quite common to hear people say that the best cure for a hangover is to return to drinking alcohol, which of course, in the terms described above is true, but is part of a short path to alcohol dependency.

An important experiment into the tolerance effects of alcohol was undertaken by Crowell et al. (1981). They found that rats were largely unaffected by injections of alcohol when it was administered in an environment that they had come to associate with the administering of alcohol previously. This suggests that tolerance is not only affected by repeated use, but by the environment in which the drug is taken, if you only ever drink in a pub then drinking the same amount at home would have a significant effect. Similarly, if you get used to drinking at home, then it will take ever larger amounts of alcohol to have the same effect. Particular problems arise for those people that get used to drinking in all environments.

Further tests have shown that it is not purely the desire to remove withdrawal symptoms that motivates alcoholics to drink more, but is more closely related to the pleasurable effects that they derive from continued engagement in this activity. In order to understand this we need to return to the positive incentive theory quoted in the second chapter. It seems that alcoholics and drug addicts alike are primarily seeking out the pleasurable effects of their drug, although the theory does acknowledge that the suppression of withdrawal symptoms is an associated (but secondary) consideration. In fact Robinson and Berridge (1993) argue that it is the anticipated pleasure of the drug that is a major motivating force in the activities of most addicts. Such positive incentive theories stem from the findings of Olds and Milner's (1954) study of rats given the opportunity to electrically stimulate areas of the brain that mediate the pleasurable effects of rewards (further discussed in Chapters 6 and 9). More recent evidence (Chen, 1993) has suggested that self-stimulation of the brain has an effect on motivated behaviour and drug addiction. This research suggests that it is the activation of the **mesotelencephalic dopamine system** (a system of dopamine-producing neurons that project into the telencephalon area of the brain), which causes certain behaviours to provide a pleasurably rewarding sensation. Such findings help us to see what the specific rewarding properties of certain behaviours and drugs might be and may in the long run lead to ways of controlling such behaviours.

It may just be though that the disinhibitory effect of alcohol provides a stimulus to use it as an escape from the problems of daily life. Unfortunately for a great many chronic alcoholics the continued abuse of their drug causes greater misery and unhappiness in their lives than they ever experienced previously.

Chapter summary

In this chapter we have considered the factors involved in the identification of thirst, looking at environmental, cultural and social factors as well as physiological ones. We have looked at the application of homeostatic mechanisms to thirst, particularly the need to maintain a balance between the intracellular and extracellular compartments. Two types of thirst have been identified, osmototic and volumetric.

Osmotic thirst occurs when one of the water compartments becomes hypertonic (due to an increase in solutes) and consequently needs to draw more water into it. Osmoreceptors in the brain appear to be responsible for the initiation of drinking behaviour and water retention, although the evidence is not clear and mostly conducted on rats.

Volumetric thirst occurs due to the loss of water volume through bleeding, for example, which needs to be replaced very quickly. Similar receptors to those identified above in the heart and brain respond to the loss of water volume and lead to drinking behaviour.

Although these processes provide an explanation of the *need* to drink, they don't necessarily provide an explanation of the *desire* to drink (spontaneous drinking). Spontaneous drinking appears to be influenced by factors other than physiological processes, including habit and socialisation.

The desire for alcohol can be explained by its neurochemical effects, and alcoholism can be largely explained by the physical dependence theory of addiction. Continued use of alcohol can lead to tolerance, dependence and withdrawal, which make it very difficult to stop.

Review exercise

Without referring back to the text, provide definitions of the following terms.

Osmosis –

Isotonic solution –

Sham drinking –

Volumetric thirst –

Osmoreceptors –

Spontaneous drinking –

Baroreceptors –

Antidiuretic hormone (ADH) –

Further reading

Wagner, H. (1999) *The Psychobiology of Human Motivation*. London: Routledge. A useful source for the whole section on motivation and it contains an excellent chapter on homeostasis and drinking.

Wong, R. (2000) *Motivation: a biobehavioural approach*. Cambridge: Cambridge University Press. Chapter 6 offers a more detailed analysis of the drinking behaviours explored in this chapter.

5

Psychological theories of motivation

Incentives and needs
Maslow's hierarchy of needs
The need for achievement
Expectancy theory
Goal-setting theory
Chapter summary

Incentives and needs

The first chapter suggested that whilst behaviour may be driven by biological factors, this can only explain some of the more basic examples of behaviour. In order to explain the range of behaviours that humans display, we must either take the **reductionist** approach suggested by **instinct theory,** i.e. that there is an instinct for each and every one of these behaviours, or we must take the view that there are other factors involved. If we take the latter view, it may be that certain forms of behaviour are encouraged because they provide us with some form of satisfaction or reward, in other words there is an incentive to engage in such behaviours.

Incentives offer up the possibility that we *are* driven towards certain forms of behaviour, not by biology but by other needs that must be fulfilled. Such needs are related to cognitive factors and take greater account of external factors, for example, in the study of motivated behaviour.

Maslow's hierarchy of needs

Abraham Maslow comes from the humanist perspective within psychology and as such he provides an apparently individualistic approach to the issue of motivation. Rather than looking at internal biological factors as the driving mechanism for behaviour, he is interested in the cognitive factors that push people towards certain forms of behaviour. Maslow was concerned to identify the needs that 'pushed' people into behaviour beyond the most basic fulfilment of survival needs. He proposed a hierarchy of needs with basic survival needs at the bottom and other psychological needs towards the top (Figure 5.1). According to this view, humans have evolved beyond the requirements of simple survival and are now driven towards greater achievements; the highest of these is **self-actualisation**. This is the desire to achieve all that it is possible for an individual to achieve, which is present in all humans (but no other species).

Maslow qualifies his argument with four important points:

1. The needs at the bottom of the hierarchy must be fulfilled before the needs higher up can be considered; i.e. you must take care of your physical needs before you can begin to explore your cognitive/achievement or **aesthetic needs**. A lack of food may make it difficult to concentrate on your work.
2. Although all of these needs are present in all humans, all of the time, they are linked to development, such that one need may predominate over another at certain stages of development. For example, babies will be more concerned with the satisfaction of basic needs (food), than with the need for achievement.
3. Whilst needs at the bottom of the hierarchy are physiological, the higher up the hierarchy one goes the less they are related to biology and the more they are related to life experience, which will inevitably be different for each individual. This partially explains why it is that some individuals will achieve more than others will (because they have greater opportunities to do so).
4. There are significant personality differences that will help to explain why some individuals are more capable of achieving more than others. Maslow identifies a list of self-actualisers as well as a list of characteristics that such people possess. His list of achievers

included Einstein, Abraham Lincoln and William James (regarded by some as the first psychologist).

His list includes such characteristics as:

- A greater understanding of new/uncertain situations and life experiences
- The ability to react to changing circumstances
- Total acceptance of oneself and others for what they are
- Resistant to the norm, but not deliberately unconventional
- Concerned for the welfare of others
- Able to develop satisfying personal relationships
- Highly creative
- Sound moral/ethical standards

(And presumably a good sense of humour as well.)

This is by no means the full list of characteristics suggested by Maslow, which is why he is often criticised for making unrealistic demands on self-actualisers, which makes it very difficult for most mere mortals to achieve this lofty position.

Apart from the characteristics associated with self-actualisation (above), Maslow also proposed behaviours that could be associated with the fulfilment of these needs. Behaviours that were related to survival needs were called '**deficiency or D-motives**', behaviours related to any need which required fulfilment for its own sake were called '**being or B-motives**'.

Maslow provided some examples of the type of behaviour or approach to life that would lead to self-actualisation:

1. Taking responsibility
2. Being honest
3. Being prepared to try new experiences
4. Listening to your own feelings
5. Being prepared to be unpopular

Evaluation

- One of the main criticisms that is most often levelled at Maslow is his over-expectation for self-actualisation. His criteria mean

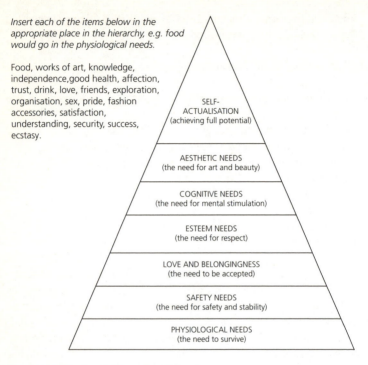

Insert each of the items below in the appropriate place in the hierarchy, e.g. food would go in the physiological needs.

Food, works of art, knowledge, independence,good health, affection, trust, drink, love, friends, exploration, organisation, sex, pride, fashion accessories, satisfaction, understanding, security, success, ecstasy.

SELF-ACTUALISATION
(achieving full potential)

AESTHETIC NEEDS
(the need for art and beauty)

COGNITIVE NEEDS
(the need for mental stimulation)

ESTEEM NEEDS
(the need for respect)

LOVE AND BELONGINGNESS
(the need to be accepted)

SAFETY NEEDS
(the need for safety and stability)

PHYSIOLOGICAL NEEDS
(the need to survive)

Figure 5.1 **Maslow's hierarchy of needs**

that it is probably impossible for all but a few to achieve self-actualisation, which according to him is an inherently human need.

- Look back at the list of characteristics and behaviours associated with self-actualisers, if this were true then it would either be possible for no one or possible for everyone, either way it doesn't provide an adequate explanation of motivated behaviour.
- Even if you accept that a small number of people display some of the characteristics in Maslow's list, it is highly unlikely they would have them all, e.g. some of the most successful people have difficulties in maintaining good personal relationships.
- But perhaps this would mean that they are not 'true' self-actualisers and therefore could not be included in the list, which brings us back to the problem of who would be included in such a list. If we are to take account of the variety of fields of human endeavour

and include in this the sporting, as well as the intellectual (as I am sure we must), it would then be likely that very few people would fit easily into the list.

- Apparently Maslow had a few selected individuals in mind when he was drawing up his list of characteristics and behaviours and hasn't taken into account the full range of possibilities for human achievement.
- Similarly, he doesn't seem to have taken account of the possibility that people who make only small achievements in their lives may feel satisfied and fulfilled and believe, or indeed truly have achieved their full potential. This may be due to the restrictions placed upon them by their social position or background.
- However, what Maslow has done is try to explain human motivation in a way that takes account of individual differences in personality and that is an advance on the purely biological or reductionist approaches of some personality theorists.
- Maslow accepted that few people would achieve self-actualisation due in part to individual personality differences but also due to social and environmental barriers that would prevent this, but he did believe that it was possible for everyone to have brief periods in their lives when they do have the feeling of satisfaction and fulfilment that would accompany self-actualisation (he called these *peak experiences*).
- Maslow has been criticised for suggesting that you must satisfy basic physiological needs before it is possible to fulfil the higher needs. However, without these basic needs nothing else would be possible.
- Furthermore, Maslow himself recognised that some high achievers would go without these basic needs for long periods of time in order to devote themselves to their work, e.g. an artist who works non-stop on his masterpiece.
- Although the nature of his rather vague categories do not lend themselves to precise experimental testing, Maslow (1968) did conduct interviews with a number of very successful people (in their own field). He found support for the view that during these *peak experiences*, such people were not concerned with deficiency needs but only with the satisfaction that comes from the fulfilment of being needs. This is supported by the statements of top sporting performers who report 'losing themselves in the ecstasy of their

performance'. No doubt similar to the *focus* suggested more recently by top sprinters (Lewis and Christie).

The need for achievement

The history of human society is full of examples of the achievements and successes of great individuals (great athletes such as Carl Lewis, entrepreneurs such as Richard Branson and political leaders such as Martin Luther King). These people have apparently been driven towards their goal by a variety of factors. However, whether it was the desire for a focus in one's life, or a desire for innovation, or just a dream, these individuals seem to have a greater desire for achievement than the mass of 'non-achievers'. But is this necessarily the case? Could it not be that everyone has an equal desire/need for achievement, but that society values some achievements over others?

These issues inevitably lead us towards some difficult questions, which we must answer if we are ever going to understand the problem of achievement fully.

Does everyone have the need to achieve and succeed?
Is this need the same for everyone, or do some have a greater need than others?
If this need exists, where does it come from?
Are we driven towards achievement by internal or external factors?

McClelland (1961) was one of the first to investigate the need for achievement, as it was included in his extended list of needs (described earlier). He suggests that the desire for achievement in a society could be measured from the kind of **achievement imagery** presented to children. Achievement imagery refers to the way that the ethos of society is transmitted to children through the stories and images that are made available to them. If these images are concerned with the need for achievement then they will grow up with this view, which in turn would be reflected in measurable factors such as economic growth. This issue is undoubtedly important at a societal level but doesn't necessarily help us to explain the differences in achievement between individuals.

Working separately McClelland and Atkinson borrowed the idea of **projective tests** from psychoanalysis, and developed the Thematic

Apperception Test (See box below) that involved showing a picture to their participants and asking them to describe what they could see. From this they were able to identify their motives, for example, hungry people would provide explanations based around food. From their tests they were also able to identify those individuals with a greater need for achievement (nAch), such people are dominated by the desire for success and have certain qualities that make them more likely to succeed, e.g. problem-solving ability, but first and foremost, such people are ambitious.

The conclusions of McClelland and Atkinson's work have been most influential in the areas of work and sport, providing answers to some of the questions posed earlier as to why it is that some people achieve more than others.

Participants would typically be asked to look at a picture/scene of people involved in some activity for 15 seconds. They would then be asked to answer a series of questions, such as:

(a)   What is happening? Who are the people?
(b)   What past events led to this situation?
(c)   What is wanted by whom?
(d)   What will happen next? What will be done?

Motivation is then assessed and scored according to their responses, e.g., if the responses make reference to superior/subordinate relationships, or one person trying to control another, this indicates a desire for power and achievement.

If you were to use these type of questions with the picture shown, what kind of answers might come? What do you think is happening? What has led to the boys being in the situation that they are? Do they want anything, or does someone want something from them? What is going to happen next?

Clearly, an ambiguous picture such as this would provide a range of possible answers to these questions, depending on the individual motivations of the people answering them.

There could be an argument going on, or maybe the boys are just involved in a game of football. Maybe they are watching someone involved in a dispute, or maybe they are waiting for a dog to return a stick.

continued . . .

Figure 5.2 McClelland's thematic apperception test

Application to sport

The study of the psychological basis of motivation has become increasingly important in the sports arena. Although the pursuit of sport psychology has been going on since the 1920s, it did not really take off in Europe until the 1960s. At a time when much of psychology was concerned with **behaviourism**, Coleman Griffith was initiating the study of the personalities of sportspersons. This shift continued through the 1960s with the rise of humanism and the application of other theories to sport became more popular (including achievement motivation).

As mentioned above McClelland et al. (1953) provided much of the early research into these factors and concluded that any attempt to understand a person's motivation to achieve must take into account both the personality and the situation that the individual finds him/herself in, so explaining the personality factor that drives people from disadvantaged backgrounds to achieve in spite of their situation.

Atkinson (1964) adopted this position and showed how the relationship between the two could be understood with reference to two specific motives:

1. The motive to achieve success.
2. The motive to avoid failure.

These motives are aspects of our personality and as such can be seen to be unequally distributed amongst the population. Those with a stronger motive to achieve success:

- actively seek out challenges and persist for longer at them;
- strive for excellence in their own performance;
- enjoy performing in front of others and value their feedback;
- (and perhaps most importantly) are not afraid of failure.

Unfortunately, but perhaps to be expected, those with a strong motive to avoid failure are almost exactly the opposite. They avoid a challenge, choosing either a very easy opponent or a very hard one, dislike evaluation and feedback from others, blame their failure on external factors and are generally preoccupied with the thought of failure.

In relation to sport, those individuals that are high in achievement motivation are often regarded as more competitive and it is this difference that is most often cited by sporting performers when explaining the reason for success and failure. How often have you heard a top sportsperson say that they won because they 'wanted it' more than their opponent, or that they were 'hungrier' than their opponent?

This notion of competitiveness has been researched with the use of the Sport Orientation Questionnaire (SOQ) developed by Gill and Deeter (1988), and is made up of 25 questions which measure:

- competitiveness – the desire to achieve success;
- win orientation – the desire to beat others;
- goal orientation – the desire to achieve personal goals.

Unsurprisingly, it was found that: sportspersons scored higher than non-sportspersons in most areas; sportspersons concern themselves more with performance than outcome. More surprising perhaps are the findings that males scored higher than females on competitiveness and win orientation; and that females scored higher than males on goal orientation.

This research not only provides insights into the reasons for some people becoming involved in sport in the first place, but also begins to show the relationship between intrinsic and extrinsic motivation. Intrinsic motivation stems from the achievement of personal goals, whilst extrinsic motivation stems from the achievement of success and the rewards that go with it. These issues will be explored further in the next section, but relate to sports psychology through the ideas of learning theory, which suggests that the motivation for behaviour comes from the expectation of receiving some form of **reinforcement**.

Sporting activities have the potential for many rewards, some of which are tangible, such as a trophy; some are less so, such as praise or the feeling of a good performance. However, it is difficult to imagine any but a few people maintaining a high level of personal motivation in the absence of any positive feedback or external success (such individual differences will be explored further in the next chapter).

Expectancy theory

The desire for achievement and the role of incentives in this are particularly important in relation to the world of work. Maslow's ideas seem to suggest that our desire for achievement is mostly related to the need for **intrinsic** satisfaction rather than the need for external rewards, such as food or money.

However, a more complete explanation must at least consider the possibility that people will be more motivated by rewards and bonuses offered to them. Sometimes called *incentive theory*, **expectancy theory** is the view that we are motivated to work by the expectation of some form of reward.

Vroom (1964) put forward a version of this theory, in which he suggests that the likelihood of adopting a particular behaviour will be determined by:

- The desirability of the outcome of an action.
- The perceived relationship between the action and the outcome.

Imagine, for example, going to work for nothing more than the satisfaction of doing a good job and that on completion of that good work you were asked to consider the feeling that you get from doing a good job as your reward.

Would you do it?
Would you do a good job?
What would make you more likely to do a good job?

Progress exercise

The debate between **intrinsic** and **extrinsic motivators** (satisfaction versus reward) is an issue for both employers and employees alike. Will employees be motivated to work hard and put in their best effort purely by the promise of payment or will they be equally (or more) motivated by the satisfaction and pride gained from doing a good job? Since industrial relations began there has been an important interaction between the two, such that workers and unions have not only pushed for more money, but have been concerned for better working conditions as well (in themselves they provide no apparent extrinsic reward).

These factors have become very important in the field of work psychology and another version of this theory has been put forward by Porter and Lawler (1968), who agree with Vroom to an extent, but add the issue of traits and abilities as an important factor.

According to them, successful managers display inner-directed personality traits, such as independence and decisiveness, whereas unsuccessful ones display other-directed traits, such as adaptability and co-operation.

Pay though remains one of the more obvious forms of reward that can be offered in the workplace and it is particularly appropriate because it possesses some very important characteristics:

- Its *importance* is valued.
- It has significant *flexibility*.
- It can be offered *frequently* without losing its value.
- It has high *visibility* and its effects can be judged easily.

(Lawler, 1981)

This means that attempts to increase motivation will most often be related to pay.

A topical and rather controversial application of this has been the introduction of **performance-related pay** (PRP), which has presented itself in a number of forms over the years from simple bonuses to profit sharing. It is believed to have started at the very top of organisations with extra financial rewards offered to executives for better company performance, the premise for such rewards being that they will increase the motivation to work harder at improving the efficiency/productivity of the organisation. However in more recent times the size of these rewards and the justification of them has been questioned, not only by workers and unions but also by government (particularly in the case of former state-owned utilities).

PRP is spreading to wider sections of the workforce (based on the same premise outlined above) but is causing problems for management–worker relations, as it is often seen as a replacement for the normal inflation-linked wage increases and it is sometimes difficult for all workers to take advantage of it. The problem with this type of scheme is that performance is often very difficult to measure at an individual level and a wide range of other factors confounds the performance of the organisation.

Progress exercise

What other factors are being referred to here?

Think about your own experience of school/college, to what extent can the activities of the teacher be said to be responsible for the achievement of the students in the class?

Create a pie chart to show the relative importance of each factor that you identify, including the performance of the teacher.

Think about this in relation to the work situation in general and make a list of other factors that could hinder any employee's performance.

Application to work

- The idea of expectancy has been applied to the work situation by McGregor (1960), who focused on the expectancies or attitudes of the employer/manager towards the employee. McGregor proposes two theories (belief systems in this case), which lie at the extremes of the possible attitudes of the employer/employee relationship, but are to a large degree influenced by the logic of expectancy theory.

1. *Theory X* suggests that employees are lazy, unreliable, not to be trusted and only motivated to work by the pay or the threat of losing it (extrinsic motivation).
2. *Theory Y* suggests that employees gain satisfaction from work, are trustworthy, thrive on a challenge and are motivated by the satisfaction gained from doing a good day's work (intrinsic motivation).

The first theory encourages employers/managers to take a hard line and control the workforce by the promise/threat of removal of rewards. The second theory encourages the employer to work with the employee to provide the possibility for internal motivation.

- Employers now recognise the need to minimise dissatisfiers (anything that causes an employee to feel unhappy) in the workplace and maximise satisfiers (Herzberg, 1966), in order to create a happy, motivated workforce. Herzberg interviewed engineers and accountants about the effects of feelings of satisfaction and happiness on their work and found that people have two sets of needs; to avoid pain and to be able to grow psychologically (not too far away from Maslow's view of self-actualisation). Herzberg suggests that there are two sets of factors influencing motivation at work, one set he calls motivators and the other hygiene factors. Motivators include achievement and recognition, whereas hygiene factors focus more on pay and conditions.

Goal-setting theory

This movement towards a greater recognition of cognitive factors in the workplace was taken further by Locke (1968) in **goal-setting theory**. According to Locke, 'a goal is what an individual is trying to accomplish' (Locke et al., 1981).

In order to provide motivation in the workplace, a worker must have a realistic goal which will, once achieved, provide a sense of accomplishment. Research into the effect of goal-setting has shown that it can improve the cost control, quality control and satisfaction of the workers using it (Ivancevich and McMahon, 1982).

However, a review of research by Locke and Latham (1990) has proposed that a number of important variables influence the success of goal-setting:

1. Difficult goals are more successful than easy goals, as long as the workforce is committed to achieving them.
2. Specific goals are more successful than general goals. A general 'we must all work harder' is not precise enough to motivate someone to work harder at a specific task.
3. Feedback on performance is essential at all times leading up to the achievement of the goal.

It is this kind of research that has helped to shape job design programmes in a number of areas of work over the course of the last 20 years.

But the effect of **impression management** on performance as well as the different requirements and effects on individuals of arousal complicate these issues. It could be that the intrinsic and extrinsic rewards for behaviour are so arousing that a person's performance is impaired, or it may be so difficult to achieve that very few people bother trying.

Further problems for psychological theories based purely on achievement motivation occur when we consider the need for control. This need can range from the general need to be in control of your work and life to the more specific psychological need to be in charge of your appearance and performance.

Imagine you have been given a particularly difficult essay or assignment to complete (you may be working on one right now and have decided to use this book to help you). You will, inevitably, feel aroused (not in a pleasant way, more in a 'fight or flight' kind of way) at the thought of having to do this. But no doubt you will also be concerned at how you will appear if:

(a) You are not able to finish on time and everyone else is.
(b) You finish but it isn't very good.
(c) You finish on time but no one else does.

In each of these three scenarios you are faced with a dilemma that concerns your need to be in control of the situation and to make yourself appear in the best possible light.

If we are to believe Maslow and McClelland then the solution is simple. We will put our best efforts into the work in order to achieve our full potential, assuming we have also managed to fulfil the more basic needs in the hierarchy that is. But will we?

In relation to the three scenarios suggested above, identify any factors that might make you do less than your absolute best to complete the task.

Progress exercise

The need to feel in control of a variety of situations is strong in us all and may lead us to make decisions that would appear counter-productive, but could in fact be very useful to us in a number of ways: to make/keep friends, to maintain an image that we regard as desirable, to be able to blame someone/something else for our inadequacies.

Chapter summary

This chapter has considered the role of incentives and needs in motivated behaviour, by exploring the psychological, rather than physiological basis of behaviour. Maslow's humanist view of motivation has been considered, based around the basic (survival) needs and higher (psychological) needs of all individuals in society. The need for achievement has been identified as an important driving force in a number of motivated behaviours, particularly work and sport. This need has been considered as part of an explanation for individual differences in motivation. These explanations in relation to sport have focused on internal factors, such as the desire for success and the desire to avoid failure. In relation to work, expectancy theory has looked at the debate between the importance of intrinsic and extrinsic factors in work motivation (satisfaction versus reward). This debate has stimulated a lot of research into the best way to motivate people in the workplace and consequently, the creation of job design and management training programmes, all intended to get the most out of the workforce.

Make a table for each theory as follows:

Name of theory, proposer and date	Key concept	Evidence supporting	Evidence against

Further reading

Wagner, H. (1999) *The Psychobiology of Human Motivation*. London: Routledge. Chapter 9 is particularly good for cognitive/social motives.

McKenna, Eugene F. (1994) *Business Psychology and Organisational Behaviour*. Hove: Psychology Press. An excellent review of the factors involved in work psychology. Chapter 2 is most relevant to the theories outlined in this chapter.

Coolican, Hugh (1996) *Applied Psychology*. London: Hodder & Stoughton. A useful overview of the main areas of applied psychology with chapters on sport, occupational and educational all being relevant to the study of motivation.

6

A combined approach to motivation

Arousal
Needs and drives
Drive reduction theory
Pain and pleasure
Opponent process theory
Optimal level of arousal theory
Chapter summary

Arousal

This chapter will look at one of the 'grandest' theories in the whole of psychology, i.e. a theory that attempts to explain all aspects of behaviour, as well as a more recent theory that helps to explain some of the individual differences in motivated behaviour. This chapter will attempt to bring together the psychological and physiological influences on behaviour by exploring the relationship between arousal and motivation.

Fight or flight

A useful starting point for understanding the effects of arousal on behaviour is to refer back to the instincts and drives mentioned in Chapter 1.

In certain situations an animal will be faced with a threat of danger. In such situations the animal will react in one of two ways, it will either prepare to fight (or actually fight), or it will run away. In some way these responses are instinctive and are based around naturally evolved responses to these dangers. However, to some extent they are also learned and/or involve cognitive processes.

If we regard the animal's response as simply a *reaction*, then it is purely biological. If though, we regard the response as a *decision*, then it must also be psychological. Silber (1999) uses the example of a small mouse faced with a much larger predatory cat. In this situation the 'sensible mouse' will probably decide to run away as he knows that the cat would most likely tear him to pieces (this scenario is only ever reversed in cartoons).

But, the 'sensible mouse' may still need to assess the situation and make a decision to run away or adopt some other form of behaviour that fits the needs of the situation e.g. is there anywhere to run? Will the cat see me if I stay very still? Can the cat actually get to me? This cognitive appraisal of the situation brings into question the idea that the mouse's response is purely instinctive or automatic.

It is not possible to provide an easy answer to this question, but there is evidence from physiology to suggest that this response is largely automatic and is caused by the activity of the sympathetic branch of the autonomic nervous system.

The body reacts to such situations with a series of autonomic responses that aid the 'fight or flight' response:

- The pupils dilate.
- The mouth dries out.
- The airways relax.
- Heart rate increases.
- Sweating increases.
- Glucose and adrenaline are released.
- Blood vessels constrict.
- And finally . . . the bladder relaxes (don't we just know it?).

All of these actions are aimed at increasing our ability to respond appropriately to a dangerous situation. Of course none of them would occur if we did not recognise the situation as a dangerous one, which itself relies on an accurate cognitive appraisal (this theme will be returned to later in the chapter on theories of emotion).

Progress exercise

Think back to a time when you have been faced with a situation similar to our 'sensible mouse' i.e. being faced with the threat of violence.

What was your first reaction?
How did you deal with the situation?
Have there been other, similar situations, where you acted differently?
Why?

Needs and drives

We have already seen in earlier chapters of this book that a biological need (for food or drink) can lead to a drive to restore the homeostatic balance and therefore a particular form of behaviour. According to this view, the drive is a positive 'push' towards need fulfilment and can therefore be regarded as almost entirely natural. However, if we regard the behaviour as something that is designed to reduce the drive, we must see the drive as a problem that is causing an uncomfortable level of arousal, which must be dealt with by the most appropriate form of behaviour. Hunger, thirst and cold are examples of such problems which we are motivated to deal with in order to reduce the arousal that is caused by them.

Drive reduction theory

According to **homeostatic drive theory**, behaviour is directed towards fulfilling certain biological needs.

According to **drive reduction theory** (Hull, 1943), behaviour is directed towards reducing the tension that is associated with unpleasant drives, which are themselves caused by needs arising from tissue deficit.

At first sight these two do not appear fundamentally different, as both are concerned with the maintenance of a stable internal environment. However, drive reduction theory is not simply related to the notion that biological needs lead directly on to specific forms of pre-determined behaviour. It incorporates within it aspects of **learning theory**, such that behaviour that is most successful in reducing the tension associated with drives is repeated later and is therefore learned.

In relation to the example of the 'sensible mouse', it has learned from previous encounters with cats that the best way to reduce the tension associated with fear is to run away, therefore this behaviour is repeated on a number of occasions.

In this sense arousal is not seen as a positive experience, but is in fact regarded as something that should be dealt with as soon as possible in order to return to normal non-aroused functioning.

This theory therefore combines features of homeostatic drive theory with learning theory. According to this view, the behaviour of animals and humans is learned through a process involving reinforcement (similar to expectancy theory quoted in Chapter 5) such that, if a behaviour is reinforced i.e. associated with a pleasant outcome, it is more likely to be repeated in the future.

We can see that animals put into cages or mazes are motivated to make their way out by the need for food that is offered to them upon completion. In this situation the food acts as a **primary reinforcer** (something which fulfils a basic need) for the animal's behaviour. The theory was later broadened out to include reference to **secondary reinforcers**, which can be used to reduce drive states such as money that can be used to buy food. Therefore, we are motivated to work by the same needs and drives.

The theory could even be applied to sexual behaviour as can be seen from the reduction in arousal that follows an orgasm. Therefore, sexual behaviour may be engaged in to reduce anxiety and tension and will therefore increase in frequency when anxiety or tension is high, be it alone or with a partner.

As we can see Hull's theory could be applied to almost any aspect of human behaviour, which is why it is regarded as a **'grand theory'**. According to Hull, all behaviour is influenced by a single drive force directed towards tension reduction, although he does not identify the source of this energy and believes that any bodily need would act as a source for the drive (Evans, 1989).

Evaluation

- The theory receives most support when applied to areas of homeostatic functioning. It is reasonable to suggest that when you feel hungry, you are in an uncomfortable state and therefore will need to engage in eating behaviour in order to reduce the tension. This behaviour would be engaged in routinely due to a process of learning, i.e. if we did not eat at certain times of the day we would get hungry and experience the tension. Therefore, we *learn* that we must eat at regular times of the day if we are going to avoid this tension.

- It is not difficult to see how this could be broadened out to other forms of homeostatic behaviour, which we engage in at regular or specific times of the day.

- Although Hull does not provide a specific source for the energy behind behaviour, there is experimental support for his view from a number of studies that have shown that animals will engage in specific behaviours such as eating/drinking more vigorously when they are stimulated by a different need e.g. fear avoidance (Meryman, 1952; Gray and Smith, 1969).

- Even in those areas where the theory appears strong (homeostatic needs), it has come up against strong opposition. Sheffield and Roby (1950) showed that rats will not only learn to press bars for saccharine, but will continue eating it for hours even though it has no drive reduction capabilities. It is possible though that the rat mistook the sweet taste for sugar and therefore learned to press it and carried on pressing it in the hope that it might at some point reduce the need they were feeling, but as we are not in a position to completely understand the needs and drives of rats, we will probably never know.

- Further problems for Hull's theory arise from an important study conducted by Olds and Milner (1954). In these studies it was possible to **electrically stimulate the brain (ESB)**, by placing an electrode into the hypothalamus of a male rat, which could be stimulated by the rat pressing a lever. This stimulation seemed to produce a pleasurably rewarding experience for the rat and the animal would engage in this activity repeatedly and in preference to any other form of stimulation (food, water and sexually receptive females).

- In one study Olds (1956) found that the rat pressed the lever more than 2000 times per hour in one 24-hour period, a figure which would have been higher had the rat not fallen asleep at the lever from exhaustion. If the rat were simply pressing the lever for food it would be expected to press the lever no more than 25 times per hour. It seems that the need for this stimulation was insatiable and far from being arousal reducing, was in fact the opposite.

- This evidence discredits half of Hull's theory regarding behaviour being activated to reduce arousal. The other half (learning), has similarly been discredited by Tolman (1948), who showed that rats would learn to run a maze by developing a mental map and would do so in the absence of reinforcement, or indeed hunger. Reinforcement was not therefore necessary for learning to take place.

Hull's theory could not recover from such damning criticism and has largely been disregarded in recent times as irrelevant to most forms of behaviour.

Progress exercise

Complete the table below by identifying which of the following behaviours support or oppose drive reduction theory. Explain your decision in the space provided. (One example is given to get you started.)

Behaviour	Support	Oppose	Explanation
Gambling		•	More closely related to a desire for pleasure than drive reduction
Exploring strange places			
Flying round the world in a balloon			
Playing computer games			
Going out clubbing			

It has probably become clear to you through the process of doing the above exercise that Hull's theory could be used to support or oppose just about any behaviour, which is why such 'grand' theories have often been rejected.

Pain and pleasure

Olds and Milner showed that connecting electrodes to apparent pleasure sites in the brain caused increased behaviour and later showed

Figure 6.1 All the fun of the fair? What is it that makes these rides fun? What is the dividing line between fun and fear?

that attaching electrodes to other (apparent) pain centres decreased the same behaviour.

However, there may be a fine line between pain and pleasure and some people (if not all of us) will seek out potentially painful experiences, from which we derive pleasure, as you may have noticed from some of the examples given in the previous progress exercise.

Whilst there is some recent evidence to suggest that a chemical is active in some people that causes them to engage in dangerous and painful activities, Freud had already offered a theory that could deal with this apparent contradiction, nearly one hundred years ago. Freud (1922) proposed that we are all born with two basic instincts; the libido and the death instinct, the former drives us towards pleasure and love, the latter drives us towards pain and aggression. Although Freud's work became very popular after his death, it is not so highly regarded anymore, due to its lack of scientific rigour and for only being completely accessible and understandable to Freudians.

Further attempts to explain this pain/pleasure connection have been made though and the next section considers the desirability of arousal in explaining potentially dangerous and painful behaviours.

Opponent process theory

One attempt to make sense of this link between pain and pleasure has been suggested by Solomon (1980). Whilst this theory could be regarded as more of a theory of emotion, it provides an explanation of the motivation for certain behaviour based on the level of emotion associated with that behaviour.

Solomon looks at emotions as pairs of opposites e.g. pain/pleasure, fear/relief, so that when one emotion is experienced the other is suppressed. When a potentially dangerous situation is encountered, the emotion of fear is heightened and relief is lessened, until the dangerous situation has gone away and the emotion of relief takes over and fear dies down. Consider this situation (which you may have experienced yourself at times); you are waiting in a queue to go on a new white-knuckle ride at a theme park. During your wait you feel anxious and fearful of what is to come. Once the ride is finished, however, the strong feeling of relief takes over and you become almost boastful about the ride not being that frightening. Similar situations can occur when faced with the threat of physical violence; during the threat the feeling of fear is intense, but as soon as it is over (assuming that you haven't been badly hurt) the intense feeling of relief will make the experience seem less frightening and to some extent make you more prepared to face such situations again. **Opponent process theory** is therefore, more of a long-term theory of motivation; repeated exposure to painful experiences will decrease the fear of such situations and increase the pleasure, as the feeling of relief increases. The fear associated with the situation is short-term, whilst the relief that follows lasts much longer and leads to both a distorted perspective of the past event and less fear when approaching the situation again. Solomon and Corbit (1974) studied the emotions involved in skydiving. Beginners approaching the experience for the first time feel intensely fearful, a feeling that is taken over by an equally strong sense of relief upon completion. Repeated successful jumps decrease the feeling of fear, whilst the feeling of relief increases and turns to great pleasure/elation, which provides further reinforcement.

Evaluation

- The theory has been very useful in explaining thrill-seeking behaviours, but has also proved to be particularly relevant to explanations of drug addiction. The pleasurable feeling associated with taking the drug is replaced by a moderately painful but longer lasting emotional state, which leads to the desire to return to the pleasure associated with the drug taking. Eventually, the drug is no longer taken for the pleasure, but merely to avoid the pain associated with withdrawal.
- Whilst this explanation does appear to make common sense it has received little support, Sanduik et al. (1985) found no such reaction to drug-taking and withdrawal and therefore, question the usefulness of the theory in understanding real, rather than theoretical, situations.
- Furthermore, the theory doesn't really explain the continued motivation for thrill-seeking behaviours, if the intensity of the fear associated with the situation decreases, surely the intensity of the relief/pleasure would decrease and the desire to engage in such activities would also decrease. However, this might make it more applicable to drug-taking behaviour and other intensely emotional situations e.g. love at first sight.

- Finally, the theory doesn't explain individual differences in such behaviours and why it is that some people choose/need to engage in thrill-seeking behaviours whilst others do not.

The theory that follows attempts to explain these differences, whilst providing a similar but distinctly separate theory of motivation.

Optimal level of arousal theory

Piaget proposed his theory of **cognitive development** on the basis that humans learn and develop as a consequence of curiosity, exploration and manipulation. This is enhanced further through the process of play, which on the one hand could be seen as a way of learning and practising new skills, and on the other as activity that is engaged in for its own sake (for the pure enjoyment or arousal maybe). From this point of view arousal is a basic need that is partially in-born and partially acquired.

One of the first proponents of a form of **optimal level of arousal theory** was Berlyne (1960), who believed that each situation or task would cause us to feel aroused/stimulated; the more unfamiliar the situation/task, the more aroused we feel. According to Berlyne, these situations have the effect of stimulating neurons in both the pleasure and pain areas of the limbic system, each situation will have an optimal level beyond which they will be too arousing and will therefore need to be stopped. Even so, such situations/activities will provide stimulation for each of us and thus will be sought in spite of the related danger/pain. This might help to explain what seem to be extremely bizarre behaviours. If you have ever watched a so-called entertainer eating a glass and thought to yourself 'How the hell did they realise they could do that?', well now you know – they just got bored.

This idea of an optimal level of arousal (related to in-built tendencies for exploration and stimulation), has been explored further by Zuckerman (1979). He wanted to investigate the apparent individual differences between those people that avoid unfamiliar activities and environments and those that do not feel satisfied until they have undertaken the most *extreme* forms of dangerous behaviour. Zuckerman referred to such people as '**sensation seekers**', who seem to *need* to involve themselves in activities like bungee-jumping, motor-racing, rock-climbing, and ski-boarding down a mountain (naked) in the middle of summer, pursued by a mountain lion, with raw meat attached to their genitals (stimulation indeed!).

Although the precise reason for the individual differences is not clear from this theory, it is likely that the desire for stimulation will depend on your 'normal' level of stimulation, so people who regard bungee-jumping as normal will need a greater level of stimulation (possibly similar to the last activity suggested above). Similarly, if you are in a situation, which is unusually boring or unstimulating, you may need a new more interesting activity to get you really stimulated (Hebb, 1955).

In order to understand how these activities relate to incentives, we need to consider the incentive value of specific behaviours. If the feeling that comes from bungee-jumping provides enough arousal to outweigh the likely pain that could result from this activity then there is an incentive to do it. In some ways it could be argued that overcoming the fear and anxiety of the activity might be enough incentive to take part in it.

It may be possible to argue that OLA theory is only applicable to modern life, where the possibilities for such arousing behaviours are different.

To what extent do you think this argument is true?

Try to find examples from the past of people engaging in activities that could be used to support this theory.

Progress exercise

Evaluation

- Support for this theory comes from **sensory deprivation** studies in which people are placed in a non-stimulating environment (plain walls, no sound and no interaction) for long periods. Studies have shown that when placed in such environments, people want to be released as early as possible due to the unpleasant feelings that are invoked.

- The main evidence for this comes from a series of experiments conducted by Hebb and colleagues in the 1950s, which involved placing people in a very small room with a bed, wearing blindfolds, ear covers and cardboard tubes on their arms and legs. A variety of stress reactions, including hallucinations were experienced during the experiments and each experiment was unable to continue for more than two/three days.

- Although this experimental situation could be criticised for lacking ecological validity (people do not usually find themselves in such situations), Cohen and Taylor (1972) studied the effects of sensory deprivation in more realistic environments e.g. prisons. They found that prisoners, round-the-world sailors and astronauts experience similar psychological effects.

- However, similarly powerful stress reactions are experienced by people exposed to over-stimulating situations, something that can be seen quite clearly from the high levels of stress occurring in our hi-tech society.

- At first sight this theory seems completely opposite to Hull's theory presented earlier (pp. 75–78), and it is often used against Hull to show that there are situations in which people seek out arousal e.g. roller-coasters. However, this may not in fact be the case, such behaviour may itself lead to a reduction in arousal as it opens up the possibility of releasing tension by engaging in dangerous activities, e.g. riding on roller-coasters has been suggested as a good way of reducing stress. There are a number of such examples where an apparently arousing activity could be seen as tension relieving, from sporting activities to sex.

- However, taking this line can still lead to problems because we would have to identify a need for all forms of behaviour and then show how engaging in certain activities could reduce arousal. This is problematic enough when we refer to apparently uncomplicated needs such as play and curiosity, but is particularly so if we try to apply it to more complex psychological needs such as achievement and approval. For these more complex psychological needs we would need to identify how engaging in the variety of activities that could lead to achievement and approval would reduce arousal, which may not be impossible, but it would be an almighty task.

- One of the apparent advantages of this theory is its ability to explain individual differences in motivation by reference to the different arousal needs of individuals. Zuckerman's earlier reference to 'sensation seekers' came about as a result of personality question-naires (sensation seeking scales), which showed that some people have a desire to increase stimulation, whilst others desire to reduce it (Zuckerman, 1978).

- This is similar in some respects to Hans Eysenck's (1952) introversion–extroversion scale, which measures personality on a spectrum of characteristics with extreme introverts at one end and extreme extroverts at the other.

Ogilvie (1968) discovered similar personality differences through interviews with top international athletes. They were found to have the following characteristics:

1. a desire for success and recognition
2. autonomous and domineering
3. highly assertive
4. loners
5. low levels of anxiety
6. high levels of emotional control

These last points may well explain why Evans (1989) has suggested that Zuckerman's sensation-seeking personality has more in common with the personality dimension of psychoticism, than with any other aspect of Eysenck's scale. Such people are not only impulsive and thrill seeking, but also emotionally detached and find difficulty in relating to others on anything more than a superficial level.

- Whilst this evidence is very useful in explaining individual differences, it does not help to explain why it is that all of us at one time or another have the desire to seek out such thrills, e.g. the desire to go on a roller-coaster ride. It isn't enough to refer to the kind of mood or situation variables referred to by Hebb (above), as this would only explain behaviour that occurs at the time the feeling/situation occurs (unless we say that people who live in constantly non-stimulating environments look forward to their roller-coaster ride at some later date).

- Furthermore, the theory itself is rather too much like the homeo-static theories described previously and therefore does not easily correspond to the real desires of people who seek out thrills far above what might be regarded as the optimum at different times in their lives.

- In response to these criticisms, Apter (1982) suggests that behaviour is driven by two **metamotivational states**, one is goal oriented, the other is pleasure oriented. Our desire for arousal is therefore influenced by our current metamotivational state. Therefore, arousal is 'felt' as pleasant or unpleasant depending on the activity that is being undertaken, such that high levels of arousal may be desirable when involved in pleasure-oriented activities but not when involved in goal-oriented ones.

- Apter's work is particularly useful in explaining the inconsistencies in individual behaviour even during the course of one activity. During the roller-coaster ride a person may well be in a pleasure-oriented state and enjoy the thrill of the danger that goes with it. However, if the ride began to collapse halfway round and actually became dangerous, this would switch to a goal-oriented state (the desire to get off the ride as quickly as possible) and arousal would be 'felt' as a negative experience. Apter's work enables us to see arousal as it is actually 'felt' by people involved in real experiences in the real world in a way that the simple notion of sensation seeking cannot.

A sporting chance?

As we have seen already above, there is a strong relationship between arousal and the behaviour of sportspersons.

One of the first attempts to understand the effects of arousal upon performance was made by Yerkes and Dodson in 1908. They tested the effects of electric shocks on the performance of rats and came to the conclusion that there was a level of arousal that was best suited (optimal) for the best performance of a task. This view became known as the **Yerkes–Dodson law** or the inverted 'U' hypothesis because of how it looked when represented graphically.

This theory appears to make common sense, from both our own experiences and observations of others. However, more recently the role of cognitive and personality factors have provided a multi-dimensional view of the role of arousal in sport, in particular using the ideas of catastrophe theory and reversal theory.

Catastrophe theory as developed by Fazey and Hardy (1988) questions the linear relationship between arousal and performance put forward by Yerkes and Dodson (the view that each small increase in arousal correlates with an equally small drop in performance). They argue that a small increase in arousal arising from a minor error e.g. missing an open goal, can in fact lead to a major (catastrophic) decline in continued performance if the level of cognitive (rather than physical) anxiety keeps on increasing. This extra dimension in the process allows us to see that a sportsperson's performance is not simply related to their level of physical arousal, but to how they think about the previous error and what that error does to their self-confidence.

Reversal theory proposes that our state of arousal will change rapidly during the course of a task and indeed will 'reverse' from fear to excitement as performance of the task improves. Furthermore, the theory introduces a subjective component into the debate by suggesting that different people will view the same task in very different ways. Obviously this theory is similar to the optimal level of arousal theory discussed in this chapter as it suggests that the optimal level of arousal is different for each individual, so some people can be aroused enough to become chess masters, whereas others would need to perform a high-risk task like motor-racing to perform at their best.

Chapter summary

This chapter has looked at the ways that physiological and psychological theories of motivation might be combined in order to form a more complete picture. Unfortunately, the picture that emerges from this combination either involves reducing the level of arousal/stimulation that is felt at different times, or increasing it. Even though these theories combine the physiological and psychological aspects of the other theories, they remain overly simplistic in some ways and overly complicated in others.

Hull's theory contains the most negative aspects of *homeostatic drive theory* and parts of behaviourism, which combine in a way that makes human behaviour into a constant battle against the pain of life.

Opponent process theory provides some explanation for the desirability of apparently painful activities and helps with an understanding of the psychological processes involved in drug addiction.

Optimal level of arousal theory provides a better understanding of the individual differences in certain forms of behaviour, something that may be particularly applicable to sportspersons, who need a higher level of arousal than most mere mortals.

Unfortunately, none of these provides a clear explanation of how and why the desire for such arousal occurs in the first place.

Review exercise

Compare and contrast the two main theories presented in this chapter, i.e. identify the similarities and differences between drive reduction theory and optimal level of arousal theory. One example is provided for each to help you along.

Similarities	Differences
Both emphasise the role of physiological arousal in determining behaviour.	DRT regards arousal/stimulation as negative, whereas OLA believes it is positive and desirable.

Further reading

Evans, P. (1989) *Motivation and Emotion*. London/New York: Routledge. Chapter 8 is particularly good on arousal and provides material on the theories dealt with in this chapter.

Emotion and the brain

Types of emotion

As stated earlier, attempts to create a unified definition of emotion have been less than successful. Unfortunately, there has been a similar lack of success in creating a universal list of emotions that everyone can agree on.

Part of the difficulty in this is separating emotional experiences from non-emotional ones. It is possible to argue that all experiences are emotional in some ways, e.g. eating involves pleasure, shopping often involves anger and even watching television can be a painful experience.

Of course these behaviours are not themselves emotions, whilst they may produce emotions, they are not a part of the emotional experience itself, or are they? (We will return to this issue in the next chapter.)

One of the first attempts to categorise emotions came from Wundt (1897), who used introspection to identify emotional experience in relation to three dimensions: pleasantness/unpleasantness; relaxation/tension; and calm/excitement.

In more recent times emotions have been studied by reference to facial expressions, in an attempt to establish 'universal' human emotions.

Ekman and Friesen (1975) were able to identify six such universal emotions in this way:

1. fear
2. sadness
3. anger
4. happiness
5. disgust
6. surprise

According to Ekman and Friesen these six are primary or basic emotions from which all other emotions sprout. They would regard these as the only states that could be regarded as pure emotions and nothing else. However, it is difficult to accept this **classical approach to emotions**, as it is almost impossible to say how each of these states would be experienced in different situations, e.g. you may be surprised to find friends and relatives in your house on your birthday, and you may also be surprised to see two cars crash into one another in the street, but are these the same emotions?

Progress exercise

Look at the pictures presented in (Figure 7.1); match up the six types of emotion above with each picture.

Did you find it easy?
Did the expressions fit easily with the list of emotions or were there some problems in matching them up?
Try to explain why problems might occur in identifying these/other emotions.

Whilst it may be possible to obtain a basic guide to a person's facial expression, it is not an easy thing to judge and if you conducted the exercise above as part of a group, you may well find it difficult to agree on each one.

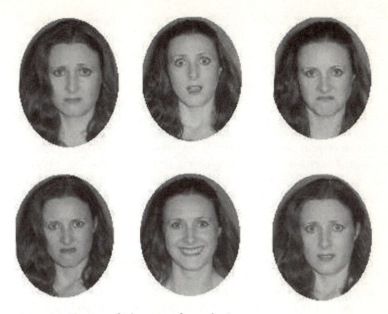

Figure 7.1 **Pictures of 'six types of emotion'**

Similarly, it is near impossible to argue that everyone who experiences one of these emotions will do so in exactly the same way as everyone else and therefore they will probably respond differently. By its very nature, a universal definition should apply to everyone everywhere in the same way. Given the nature of emotions, this is unlikely to happen and some other way of defining examples of emotions must be found.

This simple list of emotions may well provide us with a basic picture of types of emotion, but it still ignores the vast majority of emotions that exist and therefore, most of the thoughts and feelings that people experience in their daily lives.

A fresh approach to the study of emotions was provided by Fehr and Russell (1984). They asked 200 Canadian college students to provide a rating for a list of words in order, from the best example of an emotion to very poor examples. Unsurprisingly love was chosen as the best example, followed by hate, anger, sadness and happiness. Some of the poorest examples were rated as lust, pain, hunger, hope and pride. However, given that the researchers provided the students with a list of words that they considered emotions, they may well have missed some that the students themselves regarded as important emotions, making the list invalid. Perhaps they should have asked the students to come up with their own top ten, in the same way that you were in the first chapter of this book. Nonetheless, based on this categorisation and in consideration of similar points to those raised earlier, Fehr and Russell suggested that there is no such thing as a pure/basic emotion that could be separated off completely from a non-emotional state. The truth is that most physical states could be labelled as emotions depending on the situation (Parkinson, 1995).

This rather more relativist approach to the study of emotions could be applied to the study of prototypes put forward by Rosch (1978). A prototype is a typical example of what something is like. In order to understand what is meant by fear we will hold a prototypical example in our heads, but this does not mean that anything that fails to meet that prototype exactly does not count as part of that category. On the contrary the prototype merely provides the central features of the category, which all specific examples can be measured against.

You may have experienced a situation in which you have told someone that you feel happy and they have replied 'you don't look very happy'. They were obviously measuring your outward signals against a prototype of what 'being happy' looks like. This suggests that people can use facial expressions to hide their true feelings, something which all of us have probably done at some time or another.

So how do you know if that person smiling at you is really doing so because they like you or because they are trying to hide their feelings?

Duchenne (a French anatomist) was the first to study the use of the 'false smile'. He stated that a smile of true pleasure could be distinguished from a false one by studying the muscles involved in smiling. The two muscles used are the *orbicularis occuli*, which encircles the eye and pulls surrounding skin toward it, and the *zygomaticus major*, which pulls the corners of the mouth up.

Duchenne argued that only the latter of these two could be voluntarily controlled and that the former only occurred during genuinely pleasurable experiences. Lack of movement around the eyes suggests a false smile; appropriate movement suggests a genuine one, or what Ekman calls a '**Duchenne smile**' (Ekman and Davidson, 1993). So, if you want to find true friends or admirers, watch their eyes;

in this case they are the windows to the heart and mind as well as the soul.

This mismatch between how you feel and how you look suggests that there are physical properties of emotions that are not necessarily linked to behavioural signals. It may be productive therefore to identify the specific physiological mechanisms that are involved in our experience of emotion.

Brain mechanisms

Emotions are not only experienced, they are reacted to. These physiological reactions involve changes in the autonomic nervous system, which may be the basis for the 'feeling' of emotion. Alternatively this feeling may be based around specific areas of the brain, which in turn control our physiological responses.

The ANS and emotion

The sensations that occur during emotional experiences are related to ANS activity: sweating, increased heart rate, exaggerated breathing etc. If you have ever experienced a 'close shave' in a dangerous situation, you will have experienced some of these reactions. For many people these are regular feelings associated with everyday experiences e.g. the sight of a spider or being in an enclosed space such as a lift.

The question for bio-psychologists is, whether or not these reactions are the cause of the emotional experience itself, or whether these reactions are merely a response to a feeling that is triggered in the brain, or indeed whether there are other factors involved such as the environment. This argument will be returned to in the next chapter, for the moment we need to consider the specific mechanisms involved in emotions.

The specific ANS mechanisms were discussed briefly in the last chapter in relation to the 'fight or flight' syndrome. It is worth returning to these mechanisms for a moment to see if the responses would be different for other emotions. If they are, it suggests that the ANS does have a specific role to play in our experience of emotions.

Consider for a moment another form of arousal, sex. Feelings of love/lust for another person are accompanied by physical reactions.

Think about a situation in which you have experienced these kinds of feelings for another person. Identify the physical reactions that accompanied it. Are these reactions the same for love as for lust?

The specificity of these physical reactions may provide some support for the idea that these responses are separate from brain activity and are largely automatic/purely dependent on ANS activation.

Evaluation

- Studies involving removal/severing of sympathetic activity suggests these emotions are felt in much the same way as before, even without the corresponding physical reactions.
- Further problems arise when you consider the fact that in thinking about the reactions involved in love and lust, you may have also been able to produce some of those same reactions, even without the stimulus (this is related to the role of fantasising in sexual arousal). The reactions that are experienced when you hear about a fatal train crash or when you think about looking out from the top of a tall building, all suggest that emotions can be 'felt' without the stimulus and before the physical reactions are produced.
- Therefore, it seems that whilst ANS activation does accompany the feeling of emotion, it is most likely that the feeling of the emotion can be 'felt' without this activation and must be connected to some other area of the brain.

Emotions and the limbic system

The limbic system is a collection of structures that encircle or 'border' the thalamus, which itself deals with all sensory information coming into the brain. The system is often referred to as a circuit after the work of Papez (1937), who believed that the limbic structures made up a circuit responsible for the feeling of emotion and therefore the expression of emotional behaviour (see Figure 7.2).

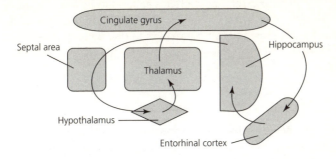

Figure 7.2 **The Papez circuit and the major structures of the limbic system**

According to this circuit, emotions begin in the **hippocampus** and are *expressed* through the activation of the hypothalamus via the **septal area**. From there they pass through the thalamus and are *experienced* through the activation of the cingulate gyrus and entorhinal cortex on their way back to the hippocampus.

This provides a marvellously simple process of activation, which is all controlled by the activity of the limbic system and was further elaborated in 1949 by MacLean, who introduced the notion that the **amygdala** plays a fundamentally important role but the cingulate cortex does not. Support for this view has come from the work of Kluver and Bucy with laboratory studies of monkeys as well as case studies of similarly affected humans.

The Kluver–Bucy syndrome

In 1939 Kluver and Bucy conducted a series of experiments with monkeys that involved the removal of the temporal lobes. The monkeys displayed a series of unusual behaviours that together have become known as the **Kluver–Bucy syndrome**:

- Putting almost anything in the mouth (including over-eating).
- Increased sexual activity (including towards inappropriate objects).
- Placidity/extremely relaxed (including previously aggressive ones).
- Lack of fearfulness, even in the presence of snakes (normally feared by monkeys).

The key to understanding these effects appears to be with the amygdala, which is contained within the temporal lobe. Lesions in this area have been shown to cause monkeys to lose their aggression and (when returned to their colony) their dominance (Kluver and Bucy, 1937).

Evaluation

- King and Meyer (1958) have shown that, whereas damage to the septal area of rats and mice increases emotional reactions, later damage to the amygdala causes the effect to be reversed.
- However, other studies have shown that septal lesions can have different effects with different species. Rats have been shown to become aggressive (Brady and Nauta, 1953), whereas mice have become increasingly fearful (Carlson, 1977).
- Such findings, showing wide variations in behaviour between different species make any suggestion of a definitive link between aggression/emotion and the limbic system difficult to justify.
- Although the Kluver–Bucy syndrome has only been experimentally tested with animals (for obvious reasons), it has been noticed in a number of human patients. Pinel (1997) cites the strange case of a man who had suffered amygdala damage due to a brain infection. He exhibited signs of placidity (although originally a restless person), he engaged in oral exploration of any objects he could get his hands on and even though he had previously displayed heterosexual tendencies, these tendencies were reversed during the course of his illness, prompting his fiancée to leave him (Marlowe, Mancall and Thomas, 1985).
- The work of Kluver and Bucy has been extremely important in the development of psychosurgery and led to the use of similar operations (amygdalectomies) on human psychiatric patients displaying aggressive tendencies (Kiloh et al., 1974).
- However, the findings of such studies and the consequent application of them to psychiatric work should not be taken at face value. Electrical stimulation of different areas of the amygdala and hypothalamus has shown that either increased or decreased aggression is possible depending on the precise area stimulated (Flynn, 1976), which might explain the mixed results found from septal lesions to rats and mice mentioned earlier.

It is by no means clear that the brain structures mentioned so far are the only ones involved in aggression, never mind the range of other emotions. Further material in this chapter will look at the role of other brain structures, including the hemispheres of the cerebral cortex.

- Even in spite of this further evidence it is questionable whether such psychologically invasive procedures should ever be carried out. Many patients have been helped by these procedures, but the full extent of them is not yet understood and on ethical grounds it opens up issues in the individual, social and political fields.

Look back over the evidence and arguments presented so far on the role of the limbic system. Based on this information (and any other arguments you can think of), construct two lists of the arguments *for* and *against* the use of amygdalectomies to control aggressive behaviour in humans.

Progress exercise

Neurochemical influences

This section is concerned with the influence of various chemicals, e.g. hormones, upon our physiological reactions and in particular in this case upon our emotions. The main area of study for the influence of biochemistry upon emotion has been in the study of aggressive behaviour. The production of hormones has been shown to be important in this area, in particular **testosterone** (a male sex hormone), which is produced in the gonads. Experimental studies have shown that castrating (removing the gonads) mice causes them to lose their aggression (Wagner, Beauving and Hutchinson, 1980). This process was reversed by the injection of androgens (male sex hormones) into the mice, which restored their previously aggressive behaviour. Similar findings have been noted in human subjects. Even though it is not possible to experiment on humans in this way, there have been studies of males in countries where castration is a punishment, which show that it causes reduced aggressive behaviour, particularly of a sexual nature (Laschet, 1973). However, it is clear that testosterone is not the only hormone involved in aggressive acts. Harding and Leshner (1972) have shown that removal of the adrenal glands in mice reduces aggression and that injecting **corticosterone** (a glucocortoid) restores the behaviour. However, glucocortoids are also connected to the production of testosterone and it is not clear whether we should simply regard the production of corticosterone as the most important feature in the aggressive personality, or whether we should see testosterone and other hormones as part of a **negative feedback system** (messages from reactions in one part of the system cause changes in the opposite direction in another part of the system) connected up to receptors in the brain that send messages to the various parts of the body.

This still leaves us with the problem though that it has thus far proved difficult to isolate a specific hormone responsible for aggressive behaviour. Leshner et al. (1973) argue that the one thing that all attempted explanations have in common is the necessity of testosterone production for aggressive behaviour.

Evaluation

- It is not always clear to what extent higher levels of testosterone cause aggressive behaviour or are themselves caused by the increased aggressive behaviour of the people studied e.g. violent criminals (Archer, 1991).
- There can be no definite answer to the influence of biochemistry on behaviour and most attempts to reproduce the sort of experiments mentioned earlier without testosterone have failed.
- It seems likely that hormones have an effect on our mood state, part of which is our tendency to become aggressive. Whether or not this can be regarded as an emotional state is less clear, although, it is just as much an emotion as happiness or sadness, which are themselves influenced by chemical reactions in the body as well as environmental factors.
- The influence of chemicals on emotion can be seen most clearly by the introduction of foreign substances into the body e.g. alcohol. This produces a range of effects depending on the amounts consumed (see Chapter 4). In small amounts it causes a feeling of high excitement and even exhilaration as the neurons that cause inhibited behaviour are deactivated whilst others are unaffected. In larger amounts all neurons start to deactivate and the effect is

to feel slow and depressed, the same kind of feeling that highly stressed people taking Diazepam (Valium) might feel.

The hemispheres of the cerebral cortex

The role of the cerebral cortex in the recognition and expression of emotion has already been hinted at earlier in this chapter, either as an interpreter of information sent to it from the ANS, or as an interpreter of information from the environment, which is then sent to the ANS (or possibly even both). Whichever way you look at it the cortex seems to play a central role in emotional behaviour.

Much of the study of this role has been in relation to the site of emotional recognition and expression within the cortex itself. The cortex is split into two halves; the left and right hemispheres, connected together in the middle by the **corpus callosum.**

The dominant view for some time has been that only the right hemisphere was involved in emotional behaviour. Past examples of patients with damage to only one side of the brain have shown some evidence for the dominance of the right hemisphere in both the recognition and expression of emotions.

A number of reported cases of people with right hemisphere damage have shown that they are no longer able to recognise or express these feelings of emotion in the same way as people with left hemisphere damage. In particular such studies have shown that lesions to the right hemisphere distort the ability to recognise facial expressions and tone of voice.

Evaluation

- Major studies by Kolb and Taylor (1981, 1988) have shown that lesions to the right temporal, right frontal and right parietal lobes do indeed distort the perception and expression of emotions.
- However, similar effects can be found in the same regions of the left hemisphere. They conclude that the recognition and expression of emotion are not lateralised, but are localised in specific regions of the cortex on both left and right hemispheres.
- It seems that the controls for the recognition of emotions are contained in the temporal (above the ears) and parietal (towards the top of the back of the head) lobes of the cerebral cortex. The

controls for the expression of emotion (particularly facial expressions) seem to be contained in the frontal, more specifically the pre-frontal lobe (forehead).

- One possible application of all of these hypotheses is the possibility that our facial expressions can actually change our mood. You not only 'put on a happy face', but in doing so you make yourself 'feel' happy.

Facial feedback

Evidence from research by Rutledge and Hupka (1985) provides support for the **facial feedback hypothesis**. They instructed participants to adopt an angry face or a happy face whilst viewing slides of similar expressions and then recorded their emotions. Regardless of what the slide showed, they felt happier when adopting a happy face and angrier when adopting an angry face. You could try this for yourselves by pulling a happy or an angry face right now. How did it make you feel?

Such ideas have spread into the world of work motivation itself and the expression of positive emotions is being recognised as a way of raising the feeling of positive emotions for both employee and customer/client. It should be no surprise to find that people in the service industry are instructed to smile at their customers as a way of making the customer 'feel' good about the experience of buying from you (look out for this next time you are at McDonald's). But it may also be (and it would be logical to assume so) that the expression of positive emotions by employers could make employees 'feel' better about their work. Briner (1997) suggests that examining specific emotional states such as pride and anger might be more useful for understanding the effects of the workplace on well being than an examination of more general states, such as stress and satisfaction.

The influence of culture on emotional expression

This chapter has considered the view that there may be a set number of universal emotions that are recognisable around the world and that the experience and to some extent the expression of emotion is also universal.

However, if we are going to explain the tendency for individuals to express emotions in certain situations then we should consider what influence socio-cultural factors have in deciding what kind of emotions we will show most often and to whom different emotions will be shown. After all, there are certain stereotypes that have been placed on the emotional expression of various nationalities, e.g., English people are regarded as being very reserved, whereas Americans are characterised as being over-enthusiastic. Clearly, any attempt to come up with a list of stereotypical emotions will depend on the point of view and indeed culture of the person drawing up the list, so it is probably not helpful to go into long lists of national groups and their perceived dominant emotions.

More scientific attempts to understand the influence of culture on emotions have been researched by a number of people, particularly comparing emotional expression in the USA with emotional expression in other more collectivist cultures, such as Japan. Indeed, Triandis (1994) suggests that individualism versus collectivism is the most important division between cultures and is therefore relevant to any investigation of differences between cultures in emotional expression. Triandis and others have suggested that collectivist cultures have an emphasis on group harmony and fulfilling one's obligation to the group, whereas individualistic cultures emphasise individual achievement and autonomy.

A number of studies (Kitayama et al., 1991; Matsumoto, 1990) have found that these cultural differences impact on emotional expression. Kitayama et al. (1991) found that Japanese participants reported significantly more socially engaged emotions (friendly feelings) than socially disengaged emotions (pride, anger), whereas amongst American participants this difference was considerably less. This is not to say that the dominant emotional expressions of Americans are pride or anger, just that they report experiencing these emotions a lot more than do Japanese. Matsumoto (1990) found that Japanese participants rated the display of disgust and sadness to in-groups as less appropriate and the display of fear and anger towards out-groups as more appropriate than Americans, suggesting that the collectivist emphasis on the group causes them to make a bigger distinction between in-groups and out-groups than Americans who value individual issues much more.

Markus and Kitayama (1994) explain this by arguing that emotional expressions are deeply embedded in culture, and as it is culture that teaches us appropriate interactions with others, these emotions become prevalent. Unfortunately, such ideas see culture in rather one-dimensional terms and as such fail to take into account the rich divergence of attitudes that are maintained amongst individuals within one culture. Consequently, further studies have not found such clear-cut differences between collectivist and individualistic cultures, nor have they found such clear-cut differences in collectivist and individualistic attitudes between participants in cultures where such attitudes are believed to predominate.

Stephan et al. (1996) compared American and Costa Rican participants and expected to find, in line with the ideas above, that the collectivist Costa Rican culture would express less negative emotions and that there would be a clear distinction between the type of emotions expressed towards family and strangers. In fact, although they did find less negative emotions expressed by the Costa Ricans, there was a reversal in the latter hypothesis, Americans were more likely to differentiate their emotional expression amongst family members and strangers. Due to their concern that culture is dynamic and that these results may stem from a change in culture amongst Costa Ricans, Stephan et al. (1998) followed up this research by comparing participants in America and Japan. The results showed a similar pattern to the earlier study in that, although Japanese participants were less comfortable expressing negative emotions in general, they did not differentiate between groups in the expression of emotions. Furthermore, although Japanese participants were more comfortable expressing interdependent emotions (showing concern for the group) than independent emotions (showing concern for themselves), than the American participants, the Americans were still more comfortable expressing interdependent than independent emotions themselves.

All of this suggests that although culture is a factor to be considered in the expression of emotion, it is very difficult to pin down to just one or two factors and may not be helped by rather stereotypical views of what a certain cultural group is like.

Factors affecting emotional expression will be considered in more detail in the next chapter.

Chapter summary

This chapter has considered the relationship between specific emotional states and various brain mechanisms. It has identified categories of emotions (in the absence of a suitable definition), and investigated the roles of the autonomic nervous system (ANS), the limbic system, biochemicals and the cerebral cortex in the experience of emotion. The ANS has been shown to be linked to the 'feeling' of emotion, but its role in the recognition of emotional states or situations has been questioned.

The recognition and expression of emotion has been shown to be more closely linked to the limbic system and the cerebral cortex as 'controllers' of our overall emotional mood and behaviour. This has been found from experimental studies of animals with various parts of their brain removed and from human patients who have suffered damage to this part of the brain.

Biochemicals e.g. testosterone, have been shown to have an important influence, particularly in the study of aggression, although it is not completely clear whether this hormone is responsible for the feeling of aggression, or whether it is produced in response to this 'feeling'.

Although there is evidence for the dominance of the right hemisphere of the cerebral cortex in emotional behaviour, recent studies have shown that the regions of the cortex responsible for the recognition and expression of emotions are in fact localised and not lateralised (they occur in specific regions on both hemispheres of the cortex).

Facial feedback appears to be an important factor in the feeling of emotion, and the facial feedback hypothesis suggests that our mood can be changed by adopting a different facial expression (you feel how you look, rather than you look how you feel).

The influence of culture on emotional expression has been considered as a link to the next chapter looking at theories of emotion. This has shown that although some studies do suggest that emotional expression is related to the culture of a society, the actual prevalence of a particular kind of emotion and the comfort experienced by people in expressing such emotions in different cultures is difficult to identify experimentally.

For each of the following statements delete the incorrect term:

Fehr and Russell found *love/lust* to be the best example of an emotion.

The 'Duchenne smile' is a *true/false* smile.

The sympathetic branch of the ANS is responsible for *deactivation/ activation*.

Kluver and Bucy removed the *frontal/temporal* lobes of monkeys.

Damage to the septal area of rats *increases/decreases* emotional reactions.

Testosterone is an important influence upon the emotion of *fear/aggression*.

Alcohol is a *stimulant/depressant*.

The dominant view was that only the *right/left* hemisphere was involved in emotional behaviour.

Major studies have found the controls for emotion to be *localised/ lateralised*.

Further reading

Pinel, John P.J. (1997) *Biopsychology*. 3rd ed. Boston, MA: Allyn & Bacon. Chapter 17. As stated previously, this book is advanced but friendly and accessible.

Explaining emotional behaviour and experience

Theories of emotion

The previous chapter considered the origins of emotion in relation to specific physiological functions and areas. In this chapter the various attempts to explain the origin, feeling and expression of emotions will be considered.

The four components of emotions; feelings, bodily changes, environmental appraisal and behaviour, will be considered in this chapter, in relation to attempts by psychologists to organise them into a pattern of events that explains how they combine to form an emotion. Each of these theoretical attempts will provide its own version of the sequence of events involved in the emotional experience and how that is transformed into emotional behaviour.

Most theories of emotion can be traced back to Darwin's theory of evolution and the publication in 1872 of Darwin's book *The Expression of the Emotions in Man and Animals*. According to this view, the expression of emotions has evolved as an adaptive function. Consider, for example, **ritualised aggression**: animals will benefit from having such clear displays of emotions as it will be clear to other members of their species what they are going to do next, e.g. a cat will arch its back when it is going to attack and will lower it to show submission. This is clearly applicable to these more primitive and overt displays, but may be less applicable to complex human emotional behaviour.

This suggests that the experience and behaviour involved in emotions may have evolved in response to the needs of humans and animals in particular environments, which might help us explain some of the clearly identifiable forms of behaviour exhibited by people in emotional situations.

Progress exercise

Using the following examples of emotions, identify behavioural messages that might be associated with them and explain how they serve to tell others what we are going to do next.

Emotion	Behaviours	What it is trying to say
Anger	Clenching your fists.	Be careful or I will hit you.
Passion		
Fear		
Jealousy		
Joy		
Excitement		
Sadness		

Unfortunately, there are many human emotions and not all of them have clearly separate behavioural messages, e.g. you may have found it difficult to clearly separate the behaviours associated with jealousy and anger in the above exercise, or indeed those behaviours associated with joy and excitement. This is perfectly understandable, but does make a pure evolutionary argument difficult to sustain. Similarly, it is not always easy to recognise the adaptive function of many of these emotions (sadness, joy), they may serve more of a social function as they help us and others behave appropriately towards one another, depending on the emotional state (Modigliani, 1971).

In many ways the evolutionary explanation of such behaviours is more motivational (goal-directed) than emotional (Smith and Ellsworth, 1985). Rather than being a true expression of emotion, behaviours such as ritualised aggression, may just be behaviour that is used by the animal to achieve a certain goal and therefore could be regarded as 'sham aggression', a form of crocodile tears perhaps.

Physiological theories

The James–Lange theory

At about the same time (1884), William James and Carl Lange independently came to the conclusion that the common-sense view of emotion was not only wrong, it was in fact a reversal of reality (as is often the case). Common sense might suggest that emotions begin with the subjective feeling (in the cortex), which is then transmitted to the rest of the body through the autonomic nervous system (ANS). James and Lange suggest that it is the ANS that responds to the stimulus, either through specific physiological changes or through muscle activity, which then sends messages to the cortex to produce the emotional feeling.

In some ways it is possible to regard this theory as 'common sensical', as it could be associated with the notion of 'gut feelings/ reactions', which are supposed to be the way we respond to some of the more basic emotions (anger, hatred, fear). Not too surprisingly then, it seems that common sense may be at odds with itself and once again we find that there is more than one version of 'common sense'.

There are numerous situations where our bodies display automatic responses that are later interpreted as a particular emotional state, e.g. when you hear a loud noise your reaction will be to jump, this puts you in a state of readiness for action.

Part of the **James–Lange** view is that different physical reactions are associated with different emotions, therefore the emotional experience depends on which aspect of the ANS has been activated, rather than just suggesting that emotions will be judged from a general level of arousal (see the **Cannon–Bard** view below).

Many of the automatic responses so far alluded to will involve a response to a particular noise (loud bangs). Some support for the James–Lange view comes from the fact that we do not respond in the same way to all of these noises e.g. banging/crashing noises will make us jump; the sound of a baby crying will make the hairs on the back of our neck stand on end; the sound of an ambulance siren will probably make the heart beat faster, but it won't make us jump. Therefore, there does seem to be some support for the view that different physical reactions lead to different emotional states. According to James, 'we do not run because we are scared, we are scared because we run'. It is this reversal that has caused the most debate.

Evaluation

Most of the critical points made against this view come from Cannon (1931) who was himself developing a physiological theory of emotion (see below).

- In spite of the claims made by James as to the instantaneous nature of the physical changes, which lead to emotions, Cannon argued that they do not occur fast enough for them to play the role that James suggests. According to Cannon, emotions are felt immediately and do not depend on the (somewhat) slower reaction of increasing heart rate or muscle constriction.
- Secondly, emotions are accompanied by a general level of arousal, which obviously result in different behaviours, but the arousal is the same regardless of the stimulus.
- Similarly, the arousal itself is not enough to produce an emotion; it depends much more on processes occurring in the brain to make sense of the emotion-producing stimulus. The heart beating faster is not the reason that we feel apprehension at the sound of the siren of an ambulance, it is because we have processed it as an apprehensive event or situation, which is accompanied by the heart beating faster.
- This criticism was based largely on an earlier study by Maranon (1924), who injected participants with adrenaline (a hormone that stimulates and maintains arousal), but this did not produce emotions. Most (71 per cent) reported only the physical reactions

(increased heart rate), whereas the rest reported an 'as if' state and provide a description of the effect, 'as if' they were scared or angry, without actually feeling the emotion. It seems that arousal is not enough, in itself, to produce these 'real' emotions.

Try running up and down a flight of stairs a couple of times. This will arouse you, it will make you sweat and your heart beat faster, but it is not likely to be an emotional experience (unless you are as unfit as I am, in which case it will produce the fear of a heart attack).

Progress exercise

- The final criticism from Cannon involves the connection between the peripheral parts of the nervous system (which the ANS is part of) and the brain i.e. the spinal cord. If this were cut it should be the case that the autonomic responses would not be able to provide the information to the cortex to produce an emotional experience.
- However, Cannon found no change in emotional experience from his own studies with cats and dogs who had these connections severed. Similar findings have been produced from studies in which human patients who have lost autonomic and somatic feedback (due to a broken neck), are capable of a range of strongly emotional feelings (Lowe and Carroll, 1985).

All of this suggests that the James–Lange theory should be confined to the pages of history as yet another idea that couldn't withstand the ravages of time, technology and the determination of its critics.

- However, some support has come from studies investigating similar issues to Cannon. Ax (1953) was able to create the emotions of fear and anger in his subjects. Fear was produced by convincing them that the recording electrodes that they were wired up to were faulty and about to give them a dangerous electric shock. Anger was produced by an accomplice of the experimenter insulting the subject. Different forms of peripheral arousal were recorded in each condition and it seems now that adrenalin is associated with fear, whereas anger is associated with noradrenalin, suggesting that different emotions are indeed formed from different physiological reactions.

- Similar findings showing the different physical reactions to different emotions were produced by Schwartz et al. (1981) in a somewhat less dramatic fashion by asking participants to recall experiences in their lives related to specific emotions. They found that anger, fear, happiness and sadness differed in relation to changes in heart rate, blood pressure and body temperature.

- Further studies into the effects of spinal cord damage have shown some support for James–Lange. Hohmann (1966) conducted surveys amongst people with spinal injuries and found that there were serious changes in the degree of 'felt' emotions. They would report feelings that were significantly diminished in comparison to the way they felt before.

- However, there is some suggestion that Hohmann's position as a paraplegic himself may have influenced these findings, although it is not clear whether this influence is for the better or worse. The fact that later studies (Lowe and Caroll, 1985) found the opposite may have been due to a reluctance to 'open up' on the part of the subjects rather than an unconscious bias on Hohmann's part. Also, it is not possible to state with any level of certainty that these subjective reports of emotional feeling are less useful than recordings of physical changes in the understanding of the emotional experience.

- Finally, it is worth returning to the starting point of this chapter, Darwin. The James–Lange theory is probably the closest to Darwin of all the theories of emotion and although it has already been criticised for its relationship to motivational states, Frijda (1986) has supported the notion of 'action readiness' as part of the emotional experience. Using self-reports of emotional states and action readiness Frijda, Kuipers and ter Schure (1989) found a strong correlation between a feeling of readiness for action and fear and anger and the opposite feeling for sorrow and despair. This could easily be related to the two branches of the ANS, the sympathetic branch is activated to respond actively, whereas the parasympathetic branch is activated for passive responses. Frijda further argues that such reports suggest an impulsive rather than controlled response in an emotional state, which is very close to the James–Lange view of an instantaneous response.

The Cannon–Bard theory

In the 1930s Cannon performed a number of animal experiments to test the basis of the James–Lange theory and to consider possible alternatives. Cannon came to the view that the feeling of emotion and the peripheral arousal that accompanied it were completely independent and although they occurred simultaneously, it was not possible to suggest that the one caused the other. Many of the arguments behind Cannon's view have already been outlined as part of the evaluation of James–Lange.

Cannon's work was taken up and supported later by the work of Bard who studied the effects of cortical damage on the emotional reactions of cats and dogs. Cannon–Bard make three important points:

1. The *thalamus* plays a centrally important role in passing messages to the cortex concerning the feeling of emotion.
2. The *hypothalamus* receives messages simultaneously from the thalamus, which are then transmitted through to the body, leading to arousal.
3. All emotional stimuli produce the same pattern of ANS activity.

Therefore, this theory is suggesting that although autonomic reactions are crucial in the process of general arousal, the experience and expression of a specific emotion is independently triggered elsewhere, in the cortex. It is this combination of general arousal and the simultaneous registering of the emotional experience in the cortex that allows us to distinguish between arousal in the presence of a bear from arousal in the presence of a member of the opposite sex.

This theory is regarded as the main physiological alternative to the James–Lange view and proved to be particularly useful, as it successfully anticipated later explanations of the role of the limbic system in emotion. Much of the support for the theory has come from the type of studies quoted earlier as part of Cannon's criticisms of James–Lange, but there are further specific studies, to show how the theory came about.

Evaluation

A number of experiments conducted by Bard have shown the importance of the role of the hypothalamus in emotion.

- Bard (1929) removed the cerebral cortex of cats and found that they were able to elicit aggressive responses, but they were unable to direct them appropriately. On the one hand they became overly aggressive to virtually any stimuli e.g. a puff of air. On the other hand these responses were expressed generally and not towards a specific person or thing.
- Later experiments, were able to elicit this '**sham rage**' (as Bard called it), as long as the hypothalamus was not removed. In such cases emotional expression was no longer possible, similar results have been shown from human patients with hypothalamic damage (see previous chapter). It seemed that the hypothalamus played the important role of emotional expression, but the organisation and feeling of emotion must be located elsewhere.
- Some support came from later studies involving electrical stimulation of different parts of the hypothalamus. Delgado (1969) elicited sham rage responses by stimulating the anterior and medial hypothalamus of cats and more ferocious attacks by stimulating the lateral hypothalamus.
- However, studies from the previous chapter have shown that stimulation of other areas of the limbic system can produce a range of aggressive responses (Flynn, 1976).
- Whilst this theory represents an advance on the James–Lange theory (in that it allows an understanding of more complex emotions being related to brain activity) in many ways it is a return to the common-sense view discussed earlier in this chapter as it ignores the crucial role played by the interaction of situational variables with all of the other complex neurological mechanisms.
- Furthermore, the available evidence does suggest that it is difficult to associate each and every emotion with a specific area of ANS activity, but there does appear to be a different pattern of activity for different emotions.

The polygraph (lie detector) test

The **polygraph** has been used to some extent in America by law-enforcement agencies. It provides a measure of ANS activity, in order to judge how such changes, during questioning, might indicate lies on the part of the suspect. In fact the polygraph measures the physiological correlates of emotions and the consequent changes in the physiological state during questioning, which indicate that someone is lying.

The problem with the test is that as we are not certain as to the guilt or otherwise of the suspect, the test cannot be regarded as completely reliable.

The usual method employed in such tests is known as the control-question technique, which involves comparing the physiological responses to control questions e.g., 'Is your name John?' (where the answer is already known), to the target question e.g., 'Did you kill Jane?' However, most people would have strong emotional/physiological reactions to questions such as 'Did you kill her?'

Psychological studies have attempted to overcome this problem by the use of 'mock crimes'. Volunteers participate in a mock crime and are then asked questions about their guilt along with other factual questions by a 'blind' interrogator.

One such study involved the use of a variation on the control-question technique, called the guilty-knowledge technique (Lykken, 1959). This involved two groups of volunteers being questioned about the mock crime, one group who had been involved and therefore had crucial knowledge of the crime, and one group who had not and therefore had no knowledge. When questioned about this knowledge a 'blind' interrogator correctly identified 88 per cent of the mock criminals as guilty, whereas none of the innocent group were judged to be guilty.

If Cannon–Bard were correct then surely it would be impossible to separate the innocent from the guilty in such studies. Therefore, if we assume that the lie detector works there would have to be differences in ANS activity depending on the specific emotion felt.

Psychological theories

The problem with purely physiological theories is that they tend to ignore the crucial role played by social, cultural and environmental factors in the perception, expression and experience of emotion. Most importantly they do not fully account for the cognitive appraisal of a situation in understanding emotions.

From this point of view it is neither enough to experience the arousal, nor is it enough to recognise a situation as arousing, both are necessary as well as an extra element. An understanding of environmental factors is required (in some situations); in order to 'feel' the experience as emotional.

Cognitive labelling theory

This theory attempts to combine the important elements of both of the physiological explanations and combine them with a psychological view that takes into account a cognitive appraisal of the situation. It is thus often referred to as the *two factor theory*, as it combines the 'emotional heat' provided by arousal with the absolutely important influence of the environment and situation.

This theory, which evolved from an important study by Schachter and Singer (1962) is called **cognitive labelling theory** as it relies on appropriate labels being applied to the situation in order to experience the emotion 'correctly'.

Of course there is no right or wrong way of experiencing an emotion, but if you are going to behave in appropriate ways then it is important that you apply the right label and therefore come up with the appropriate behaviour for the situation.

The James–Lange theory showed the need for a certain level of arousal, but failed to identify different forms of arousal for each and every emotion. The Cannon–Bard theory was able to provide a role for complex brain structures in the process based around a view of general arousal, which is useful for distinguishing between arousal in the presence of a bear and arousal in the presence of a member of the opposite sex, but still failed to include complex situational/attributional factors in the process.

Is it enough to know that you are aroused? Obviously not.
Is it enough to know why you are aroused? Again no.

Schachter and Singer have been able to introduce a third factor into this equation, which is knowing *how* you *should* be aroused.

Their classic experiment has become one of the most well known in the whole of psychology, partially for what it did achieve, but almost as importantly for what it didn't. They were interested to find out the effects of artificially induced arousal on a person's subjective feeling of emotion, depending on the situation they found themselves in. Acting on the pretence of testing the effects of a vitamin supplement, Schachter and Singer injected adrenaline or a placebo into participants who were either informed or naïve about its effects and who were either in the presence of an angry or **euphoric** (extremely happy) person. (A more detailed summary of the Schachter–Singer procedure is provided in the next chapter as a key research paper.)

Using this ingenious combination of the two main factors (general arousal and the recognition of an emotional experience) taken from the two physiological theories above, Schachter and Singer predicted that there would be a particularly strong difference between the naïve adrenaline group (2) and the informed adrenaline/naïve placebo groups (1) and (4), such that the emotional experience would be felt much more strongly by the former group.

In these situations, Schachter and Singer are observing the effect of a general level of arousal, combined with a cognitive labelling process employed by the participants to explain their feeling of arousal. According to Schachter and Singer, it is this combination that will produce an emotional experience. (The expected emotional reactions of their participants are shown in Table 8.1.)

Schachter and Singer claimed to have found just that. They reported differences between the groups (based on the participants' own reports, the experimenters' observations and measurements of pulse rates) that tied in completely with what they believed would happen. The subjects in the first condition behaved more emotionally, reported feelings of greater emotional intensity and had a larger increase in pulse rate than those in the second. With no other way of labelling their heightened level of arousal, group (1) *believed* that they were feeling emotional and consequently behaved and indeed 'felt' emotional.

This is a very 'neat' conclusion as it successfully bridges the gap between the two physiological theories and furthermore dispelled the view that different emotions were related to different forms of arousal (adrenaline affected both anger and happiness).

Table 8.1 Expected reactions of participants in each group

Group	State of arousal	Expected reactions to emotional event
(1)	Informed adrenaline	Feel very little emotions, as they are labelling the situation as adrenaline induced.
(2)	Naïve adrenaline	Feel highly emotional, as they have no other way of labelling the arousal they experience.
(3)	Misinformed adrenaline	Feel emotional (as above), although the misinformation may cause confusion.
(4)	Naïve placebo	Feel no emotions, as they have received no adrenaline.

Progress exercise

With reference to the description given above and the more detailed summary given in the next chapter; identify as many other reasons why the results may have come out as they did in this experiment. What other variables did they need to take into account?

Evaluation

- Many of the elicited emotions were not as clear cut as is first suggested and it was difficult to clearly state that the behaviour of participants in each situation was so different, being reliant to some extent on the accuracy of the observations.
- Reisenzein (1983), showed that the results were generally inconclusive, e.g. people in the anger condition reported feeling 'happy', in spite of the fact that they had been injected with adrenaline

and exposed to an aggressive model. This exposure in itself causes problems, it may not be particularly conclusive in the study of the causes of emotions to simply show that when exposed to extremely angry or extremely happy behaviour, a person will copy it (we have known this for many years).

• Furthermore, the measurement of emotional 'feeling' by the taking of a pulse before and after is neither a valid nor reliable test of a person's emotional state. It would at least be necessary to obtain a more continuous measure (Evans, 1989).

• Finally, Schachter and Singer excluded data (from participants) that they believed had somehow worked out the purpose of the experiment and were therefore, acting in ways that could have affected the results one way or another.

• This is a somewhat less than reliable approach as, of course, we cannot be certain that a person has or has not figured it out. Such factors and other methodological issues e.g., the likely effects of giving people 'any' kind of injection, the timing and dosage of the injection as well as individual differences between participants (the antics of the stooge in the euphoric condition may well have made some participants very angry), probably make this type of experiment almost impossible to rely upon or to validate.

The role of cognition in emotion

The Schachter and Singer findings can be regarded as particularly important for two main reasons:

1. Firstly, they emphasise the importance of roles, interactions and relationships between those present in the emotional experience.

An example of this is provided by a later and not quite so famous (but nonetheless interesting) experiment conducted by Dutton and Aron (1974). They arranged for an attractive female to interview unwitting male visitors to Capilano canyon in Canada. There were two conditions in this experiment, one group were interviewed on a 'shaky' suspension bridge perched high above the canyon (arousing), whilst the second group were interviewed on an altogether more stable bridge away from the canyon (unarousing). Both groups were asked to create a story based around a picture of a woman. They found that the stories created by those on the 'shaky' bridge contained a higher degree of sexual references than those in the stable condition, suggesting that the arousal had combined with the presence of the attractive female to produce sexual attraction towards the interviewer. In effect, the participants on the 'shaky' bridge had mislabelled their fear as sexual attraction. This is similar to the participants in group (2) of Schachter and Singer's study.

2. Secondly, it provides us with a novel view of how emotions come about in terms of self-attribution (Laird and Bresler, 1992).

If we are able to label the arousal that we are feeling as one particular emotion or another, based on the available information, then our emotions might be influenced by many possible sources of available evidence e.g. facial feedback, body language, and even noises and smells. This is used to strong effect by many forms of the media, from the makers of horror films, to the promoters of entertainment facilities.

Sights, sounds, situations and in some cases smells are used to encourage a particular emotion, be it fear or pleasure, which in turn will have an effect on our behaviour and encourage or discourage certain motivations.

Evaluation

- Cognition may seem at first to be the opposite of emotion. Cognition implies some form of rational evaluation or appraisal, whereas emotion is often regarded as irrational and lacking in any real thought or appraisal.

  However, the Schachter–Singer study has already shown the need to seriously consider cognitive attributions and this section jumps even further into the mire with the suggestion that cognition is the only important factor in emotion.
- Vallins and Ray (1967) were able to demonstrate the power of cognitive attributions in an experiment that involved providing participants with false feedback as to their level of autonomic arousal. In one such experiment people suffering from a fear of snakes were made to believe that their heart rates were perfectly normal upon being shown pictures of snakes. They showed less fear/avoidance later.

This suggests that autonomic arousal may not be important in many situations, but our perception of it is. Such false feedback has been shown to be effective in other therapeutic situations.

- Support for the role of cognition comes from our everyday experience of emotional states. They are entirely relevant to some object, person or situation and as such it is almost impossible to imagine them without some evaluative aspect (Parkinson, 1995).
- Whilst it is true to say that a baby will have to learn what is meant by words like fear and anger before they can be truly experienced (a cognitive-labelling process). It is also true to say that a baby will probably have to experience them first in some basic form (Leventhal, 1979).
- These points form the basis of the debate between Lazarus and Zajonc over the role of cognition in emotions. Lazarus (1984) believes that a degree of cognitive appraisal is necessary for the 'feeling' of any emotion. Opposed to this view is Zajonc (1984), who argues that affective feeling comes before cognitive processing, using the reactive emotions of babies as an example.
- Strongman (1987) attempts to provide a solution to an apparently insoluble problem by suggesting the need to differentiate between high and low intensity emotions. High intensity emotions such as fear and anger rely on a general state of physiological arousal for their expression and it is difficult to separate the two into simultaneous processes. Low intensity emotions such as sadness require no such arousal and can be experienced without the need for a behavioural expression. As there is no one type of emotion, it is necessary to recognise that there is no one dominant factor involved in the process of emotional experience.
- Finally, Parkinson (1996) provides an analysis of emotions rooted quite firmly in social psychological ground. He argues that emotions are not only social in the sense that they require an assessment of the situation and differ to some degree from one culture to another. But they are also social in that the emotional responses of others and ourselves create emotional situations that are not related to personal 'feelings'. He suggests that emotional displays can have a contagious reaction on people in a situation, which would cause them to adopt emotions that they were consciously unaware of. This view is somewhat contentious, but may represent

a clearer explanation of how emotions are experienced in our normal daily routines.

Parkinson's four-factor theory – a combined approach to emotion

Parkinson (1995) begins with an analysis of the various factors that have been considered to be the components of an emotion. From the theories of emotion which have been outlined above, he identifies four factors or variables (**Parkinson's four factors**) that might be associated with emotional experience:

- appraisal of the situation
- arousal
- facial expressions
- action readiness

Clearly, these four factors have been identified as the components of emotion throughout this chapter and also clearly, what is important in our understanding of emotion is how these four combine to produce an emotional experience.

Parkinson's answer to this question is to provide a partial synthesis of all four factors, which suggests that all four can have an influence over the emotional experience, but ultimately, whether or not they do depends on the appraisal of the situation. It is therefore, the appraisal of the situation, combined with our feelings about that situation which will have the most significant impact on the emotional experience, but this experience will also secondarily be influenced by the other three factors: our level of arousal, our facial expression and our feeling of action readiness.

Parkinson seems to give the appraisal of the situation an overriding importance in this theory, to the detriment of other factors and in that sense seems to be very closely linked to the Schachter–Singer theory. The difference though is that Parkinson does not necessarily see appraisal and bodily feedback as completely separate, indeed, he suggests that in some cases the appraisal of the situation will itself be influenced by bodily feedback e.g. attempting to make sense of why your heart is beating faster. However, he supports the conclusion of Laird and Bresler (1992), who suggest that whilst various forms

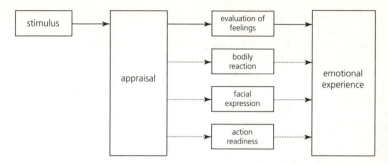

Unbroken lines represent the normal sequence of an emotional experience.
Broken lines indicate connections that are possible but not absolutely necessary.

Figure 8.1 **A diagrammatic representation of the sequence of an emotional experience (Adapted from Parkinson and Colman, 1995.)**

of bodily feedback may explain the subjective feeling of emotion, it is appraisal that explains the bodily changes that produce this feedback.

Chapter summary

This chapter has looked at possible explanations for emotional experiences, from biological and psychological viewpoints.

The biological approaches have looked at the role of either the ANS or the limbic system in the identification of emotional experiences. More psychological views have considered the particular role played by cognitive processes in the 'feeling' and expression of emotions.

The James–Lange theory emphasises the role of feedback from the ANS in the production of an emotional experience.

The Cannon–Bard theory places greater emphasis on the role of the brain and in particular the limbic system in making sense of the emotional experience prior to the feeling of emotion.

Cognitive labelling theory identifies a correct appraisal of the situation and bodily feedback, leading to the production of an appropriate label, resulting in the appropriate behavioural expression. Those who support the role of cognition in emotion suggest that cognitive labelling comes before the feeling of any emotion.

Parkinson attempts to provide a synthesis of the four factors involved in the emotional experience, but like the other cognitive approaches, emphasises the crucial role of appraisal of the situation in the experience of emotion.

Review exercise

Look back at the schematic representations of theories of emotion in Chapter 1. Label each of these as either; common sense, James–Lange, Cannon–Bard or Schachter–Singer.

Briefly explain the difference between these and Parkinson's four-factor theory.

Further reading

Pinel, John P.J. (1997) *Biopsychology.* 3rd ed. Boston, MA: Allyn & Bacon. This is particularly useful for the biological theories of emotion, as well as being amusing and accessible.

Parkinson, B. and Colman, A.M. (1995) *Emotion and Motivation.* New York: Longman. The first chapter on 'Emotion' by Brian Parkinson provides an account of traditional and current issues in psychological theories of emotion.

Study aids

IMPROVING YOUR ESSAY-WRITING SKILLS

At this point in the book you have acquired the knowledge necessary to tackle the exam itself. Answering exam questions is a skill that this chapter shows you how to improve. Examiners obviously have first-hand knowledge about what goes wrong in exams. For example, candidates frequently do not answer the question which has been set, rather they answer the one they hoped would come up. Or they do not make effective use of the knowledge they have but just 'dump their psychology' on the page and hope the examiner will sort it out for them. A grade 'C' answer usually contains appropriate material but tends to be limited in detail and commentary. To lift such an answer to a grade 'A' or 'B' may require no more than a little more detail, better use of material and coherent organisation. It is important to appreciate it may not involve writing at any greater length, but rather necessitate the elimination of passages which do not add to the quality of the answer and some elaboration of those which do.

The essays given here are notionally written by an 18-year-old in 30 minutes and marked bearing that in mind. It is important when writing to such a tight limit that you make every sentence count. Each essay in this chapter is followed by detailed comments about its strengths and weaknesses. The most common problems to watch out for are:

- Failure to answer the question set and instead reproducing a model answer to a similar question which you have pre-learned.
- Not delivering the right balance between description and evaluation analysis.
- Writing 'everything you know' about a topic in the hope that something will get credit and the examiner will sort your work out for you. Remember that excellence demands selectivity, so improvements can often be made by removing material that is irrelevant to the question set and elaborating material which is relevant.
- Failing to use your material effectively. It is not enough to place the information on the page, you must also show the examiner that you are using it to make a particular point.

Practice essay 1

Describe and evaluate two theories of emotion. (24 marks) [AEB 1999]

Starting points

This is a fairly straightforward question, requiring you to demonstrate knowledge and understanding of two theories and evaluate them. If you are familiar with more than two, the evaluation becomes a lot easier. You can describe two theories and use the others as a means of evaluating one or both of them. Be careful with this approach, however, the material must be used explicitly as evaluation (state that theory 3 is being introduced as an evaluation of theory 1 and/or theory 2). If you do not do this, the examiner will mark it as a description of a theory and only credit the best two. Sentences beginning with the words **however**, **but** or **therefore** are likely to help you in this. Other forms of evaluation could include research studies that support/oppose, methodological limitations and possible practical applications.

Remember though, starting the description of such studies/ applications with the kind of words (**in bold**) above, or such phrases as **'this theory is supported by . . . '**, will help your cause immensely.

Candidate's answer

One highly recognised theory of emotion is that of Schachter and Singer (64). They saw the stimulus for an emotional response as causing general physiological arousal (e.g. the subject experiences physical changes), and the subject interprets these changes as a particular emotion. They do this by making a cognitive appraisal of the situation and deciding which emotion is appropriate for the situation.

Schachter and Singer formulated this theory by means of an experiment. They injected their subjects with adrenaline; a stimulant often associated with emotion. They then told the subjects what they had just been injected with. One group was told the truth, one group was told a lie (that it was a different chemical and they were to expect certain reactions) and the final group was not told anything at all. The subjects were then instructed to sit in a room and wait. One of the participants, however, was a stooge, and began to act either very aggressively, ripping up paper and throwing things around, or ecstatically dancing and grinning. The subjects who had not been told what they had been injected with or had been given a false reason, were more likely to follow the man and copy his behaviour than the subjects who had been told the truth. Schachter and Singer attribute this to the subjects' attempts to attribute their general physiological arousal to a particular emotion, the stooge was simply a clue as to what the emotion was.

It has been suggested that the behaviour of the participants could be due to conformity in a strange situation rather than cognitive appraisal. It could also be true that the subjects were simply going along with what they thought the researcher wanted, but this can be said of most experiments involving humans.

Another theory of emotion was forwarded by James–Lange. Lange saw the stimulus as activating homeostatic drives within the brain. Physiological arousal occurs because the brain is attempting to reduce these drives. When this arousal is interpreted as an emotion and the person reacts with a fight-or-flight mechanism, the drive is reduced, as the person either leaves the stimuli, or faces it and reduces the emotion.

These theories could be criticised for the lack of evidence, as it is very difficult to prove whether physiological drives are the cause or the effect of emotion. They also both include physiological responses, created by the brain and the nervous system. It has been proven, however, that animals that have had their spinal cords cut can still feel emotions, but their reactions are confused.

The theories are however, quite similar, both including physiological arousal and cognitive interpretation, implying that there is a good chance that there could be truth in them.

Examiner's comments

Although the opening outline of the theory is not absolutely clear (it sounds like James–Lange to begin with), the candidate does demonstrate knowledge and understanding of the theory towards the end of that first paragraph. The reasonably detailed description of the research that follows demonstrates this knowledge further and shows that the candidate understands what was done and what it means.

The evaluation is short but accurate. It makes a couple of relevant points, followed by a useful piece of counter-evaluation. A lot more could have been done with this, however, and the candidate has really missed an opportunity to develop the methodological criticisms further and/or use other theories to provide an alternative explanation (as suggested above, although this would most likely occur at the end).

The second theory is somewhat less clear and slightly confused, as it appears to be lapsing into the (motivation) theory of drive reduction. Again though, it manages to pull it round at the end of the paragraph, but more could be done to describe the detail of this theory. Specific reference to ANS activity would help to provide greater substance to the rather abstract outline provided.

Given the extensive criticisms made by Cannon of this theory, another major opportunity for evaluation is missed at this point. The evaluation material provided is broadly relevant, but at times is rather basic (both physiological), and at other times lacks enough explanation to go beyond the limited category (spinal cord damage).

In general this candidate has demonstrated knowledge and understanding of relevant material and provided some description of the research into this area. It is rather unbalanced though and the second theory is given little mention (at least in terms of skill A). The opportunities for evaluation, mentioned in the *starting points* section, are not taken up that well, particularly the possible material on other theories. The evaluation that is provided is at times quite appropriate (but limited), at other times very basic and lacking in any coherent elaboration.

The final mark for this answer is about 7 for description + 5 for evaluation = 12/24 (equivalent to a borderline grade 'C' at A level).

Practice essay 2

(a) Describe and evaluate one physiological theory of motivation. (12 marks)

(b) Describe and evaluate one non-physiological theory of motivation. (12 marks)

Starting points

Again this is a fairly straightforward question, and as it is split into two very distinct parts, it can almost be seen as two short essays. The injunctions (describe and evaluate) are the same as the one above and therefore require the same process of showing knowledge and understanding of the theory and then evaluating it.

It is important to be sure that you are clearly dealing with a physiological theory in the first part and one that is clearly non-physiological in the second part (the phrase non-physiological has been used instead of psychological as it could be argued that the physiological theories are psychological also).

Candidate's answer

(a) One physiological theory of motivation has been proposed by Cannon. He says that the motive for any of our actions comes from a function of the body called homeostasis. This is when the body is trying to maintain a state of balance and stop any changes happening which might affect us. We use homeostasis when we want to eat or drink as our body tells us to do this to meet our physiological needs. These changes are related to the workings of the ANS which reacts to changes in our body and environment by bringing about changes in our body, like sweating when it's hot or our stomach rumbling when we are hungry. These are physical features which are not controlled by us directly, but which would happen anyway as a response to the changes talked about earlier, but they do often need an appropriate response from us to keep them in balance.

This is a good explanation of the motivation for our behaviour because these things do happen when we are hungry and thirsty, but it doesn't explain other kinds of behaviour which are not physiological. It also doesn't explain physiological factors which have no behaviour attached to them, such as breathing.

(b) One non-physiological theory of motivation is expectancy theory. This says that we are motivated by the promise of some kind of reward, which motivates us to show some kind of behaviour, e.g. footballers want to do well at football because they get paid loads of money. This kind of incentive theory has been applied to the study of work to show that we are motivated by greed and money.

The problem with this theory is that it believes that the only incentive anyone has to perform well is because of the desire for some reward. This works on the idea that we are motivated by extrinsic rewards not intrinsic satisfaction. Lots of psychologists have shown that we are motivated by internal factors like the desire for a sense of achievement, e.g. Maslow. Maslow believed that rewards like these only helped with our most basic needs and that our higher needs are achieved by self-actualisation.

A good combination of these two ideas has come from Herzberg who puts forward a two-factor theory, saying that we are motivated by two factors; one is hygiene factors which are things like pay, whereas the other is motivators, which are more like Maslow's idea of satisfaction in your job and the desire to get promotion.

Studies have found mixed results but you can't argue that people don't work for money, but we all want to achieve something as well, otherwise the work would be boring, even for professional footballers.

Examiner's comments

The splitting of this question into two parts should make it somewhat easier to structure the answer, as there is a clear divide between the describe and evaluate for each and therefore no possibility of getting the two mixed up.

However, what this candidate does show are some of the difficulties posed when you know quite a lot about one thing and a lot less about another. In this case the candidate appears to know a reasonable amount about one physiological theory of motivation and not very much about one non-physiological theory.

In fact, the situation is trickier than that because the candidate can evaluate the one that they know very little about, but not the one they know more about.

The description of the first theory is reasonable, it is lacking in quite a lot of detail and consequently ends up being rather limited, but the main features are there and so some of the important points are made. More detail on the influence of physiological drives and particularly the process involved would have helped. The evaluation of the first theory is clearly quite weak and only really makes one point, as such it is unlikely to earn more than 1 mark. More evidence for/against this theory would have helped to show how it might/might not have an influence and some consideration of the other factors involved. Consequently part (a) would achieve a description mark of about 3 and an evaluation mark of about 2 = 5/12.

The second theory is barely described at all before the candidate launches into an evaluation of it. Although a lot of candidates do suffer with evaluation, this kind of problem can occur when a candidate knows a little about a lot of theories. Clearly, it would be better to know a lot more about a slightly smaller number of theories. Fortunately, for this candidate their small amount of knowledge about different theories helps out with the evaluation. The reasonably brief knowledge that they have is used well to provide both comparison and evaluation of the theory. Using some of the evaluative phrases mentioned earlier helps to provide quite a thorough evaluation. Consequently part (b) would achieve 2 marks for description and 5 marks for evaluation = 7/12. Total = 12/24. This is the same as the last one but has obviously achieved the marks in a slightly different way, with some good evaluation of one theory and a very limited account of the other theory.

KEY RESEARCH SUMMARIES

Summary 1

Schachter, S. & Singer, J.E. (1962). Cognitive, social, and phys-iological determinants of emotional state. *Psychological Review*, 69, 379–399.

Notes

As stated in Chapter 8, this is one of the most famous studies in the whole of psychology and marks something of a watershed in the study of emotion. It is often quoted in essays, but has a rather complicated procedure and as such it is worth reviewing the detail of the study to provide a greater awareness of what you will probably end up quoting in an exam.

Introduction

The labelling of the emotional state has caused problems since the propositions of James and Lange (1884) against the belief that emotional feeling begins in the cortex and then activates the ANS. According to them, the process is reversed; emotional feeling begins in the body with ANS activity and ends in the cortex where it is labelled. This can be shown from the *fact* that different emotions involve different forms of ANS activity. The main critic of this viewpoint has been Cannon (1929), who reverts back to the original position and suggests that different emotions are accompanied by the same kind of physiological arousal. His view is supported to some degree by the work of Maranon (1924), who injected subjects with adrenaline. They only reported physical changes and felt no emotional effects whatsoever.

This leads to the view that cognitive processes related to the environment are needed in order for emotions to be 'felt'.

The problem with the Maranon study had been that the subjects all knew what the drug was and were probably aware of its effects.

Schachter and Singer combined the process of cognitive labelling with a state of physiological arousal in an experiment that took a similar approach to that of Maranon, but added the extra elements of deception as to the true effects of the injection and an environmental stimulus.

Subjects were all male college students taking classes in introductory psychology at Minnesota University. Subjects were informed that the experiment concerned the effects of a vitamin supplement (suproxin) on vision. They would then receive an injection, which they believed to be suproxin.

In fact subjects were randomly allocated to one of seven conditions; three of which placed them in a room with an increasingly angry confederate of the experiment. He complains about the injection and the personal nature of a questionnaire they had been given to fill out, finally ripping up the questionnaire in a rage and stamping out of the room. The other four conditions placed them in a room with an increasingly euphoric (ecstatically happy) confederate. He played games with stationery materials that had been left lying around; making paper aeroplanes, building towers of folders and knocking them down, etc. His finale is to twirl a hula-hoop around his arm, whilst encouraging the subject to join in.

In each condition the subject was either:

1. Informed – Injected with adrenaline and told of its true side effects.
2. Ignorant – Injected with adrenaline and told not to expect side effects.
3. Misinformed – Injected with adrenaline and told that the side effects would be itching, numbness and a slight headache.
4. Placebo – Injected with a saline solution and told not to expect side effects.

The angry situation did not include a 'misinformed' condition.

Emotional state was measured in two ways: (1) by observation through a one-way mirror, (2) by a self-report scale.

(1) The observations placed the subjects behaviour into a series of categories e.g. Angry situation – Category 1 – Agrees with confederate

when complaining. Euphoric situation – Category 1 – Joins in with confederate's activities.

(2) The self-report scale was measured in the following way:

How irritated, angry or annoyed would you say you feel at present?				
I don't feel at all irritated or angry	I feel a little irritated and angry	I feel quite irritated and angry	I feel very irritated and angry	I feel extremely irritated and angry
(0)	(1)	(2)	(3)	(4)

Similar questions were given for feelings of happiness.

Schachter and Singer had hypothesised that arousal would not be regarded as emotional in the informed condition and that no emotions would be felt in the placebo condition. Therefore, in the ignorant and misinformed conditions (but particularly the ignorant condition), the unexplained arousal combined with the emotional situation should combine to produce an emotional state.

The result would be that subjects in the ignorant or misinformed conditions would report higher levels of either anger or happiness, depending on the situation they were in, and behaving in appropriate ways when in the situation.

They claim that the results supported their hypotheses very closely indeed, providing a significant difference between conditions in excess of $p < 0.001$.

Discussion

The study confirms the view that the recognition of an emotional state relies on both physiological arousal and an appropriate labelling of the situation. However, the conclusions were regarded tentatively (even by Schachter and Singer), as they recognised the over-reliance on subjective interpretations by both the subjects and the observers. The subjects in the angry condition were reluctant to say how angry they were (they were receiving points towards their exam for taking part in the experiment). But the two observers came to an overall level of agreement in their ratings for over 80 per cent of the subjects observed.

Finally, they also recognised the possible methodological limitations that might be caused by giving the placebo injection (any injection), which could lead to some form of arousal. Indeed, the results did suggest higher levels of emotion amongst the placebo condition subjects than the informed ones (suggesting a role for cognitive factors alone). This might be accounted for by this methodological problem.

Evaluation

This experiment was not just famous, it has also been very influential in later studies of emotion. The role of cognitive factors has become a dominant theme in this area. It is questionable though that it should be, partly for the reasons outlined above, but also for the reasons outlined in Chapter 7.

Possibly the most damning criticism of all is that, by their own admission, they removed the results of five subjects who showed no symptoms of the adrenaline injection.

Summary 2

Schachter, S. (1971). Some extraordinary facts about obese humans and rats. *American Psychologist*, 26, 129–144.

Notes

This is itself a summary of the extraordinary findings of a number of pieces of research into the eating behaviour of humans and rats, conducted by Schachter and others from the 1940s and 1950s, right up until 1971. Schachter is trying to emphasise some of the differences between obese individuals and (to use his word) 'normals', whilst at the same time noting the extraordinary similarities between the behaviour of obese humans and VMH rats.

The 'feeling' of hunger

Schachter and Singer's (1962) research on emotion (above) suggested that cognitive factors played a major role in the feeling of emotion.

In order for an emotion to be 'felt', it is necessary for the individual to perceive a situation to be emotional. At about the same time Stunkard and Koch (1964) were conducting research on obesity in relation to stomach contractions. Using a gastric balloon, similar to that of Cannon and Washburn (1912), they were able to record the correspondence between actual stomach contractions and an individual's self-report of hunger. They found that in 'normal' subjects, this correspondence was high i.e. when their stomach contracts, they report hunger, when it doesn't they say that they are not hungry. In obese subjects, however, there is no such correspondence. Whether or not the obese subject reported hunger seemed to have no relationship to the occurrence of stomach contractions.

Schachter, Goldman and Gordon (1968) designed an experiment to test the relationship between actual eating behaviour and physical state, to see if there was a difference between the amount eaten by obese and 'normal' subjects.

In this test, subjects were led to believe that they were taking part in a taste test for crackers and that they could eat as many or as few of the crackers as they wished during the test. Prior to the test, subjects had been asked to miss the meal directly preceding the test, and were then either fed roast-beef sandwiches or nothing on arrival at the test. They found (as one might expect) that 'normal' subjects ate considerably fewer crackers when their stomachs were full of roast-beef sandwiches than when their stomachs were empty. However, the obese subjects ate as much – in fact more – when their stomachs were full as when they were empty. For the obese the 'feeling' of hunger in the stomach appears to have very little to do with their eating behaviour.

In order to explain this type of behaviour, Schachter looks towards data on the eating behaviour of VMH-lesioned rats to see if there are any similarities.

Extraordinary facts!

Schachter identifies the similarity between the finickiness of humans in Decke's (1971) study of the effects of taste on milk-shake drinking in obese humans and Teitelbaum's (1955) study of the effects of taste on the eating behaviour of VMH-lesioned rats. In each case the 'normal' and obese/lesioned subjects were offered food which had either been laced with quinine or not. In each case the obese/lesioned subjects ate more when it tasted good, but ate less when it tasted bad.

This led Schachter to pursue other facts about the eating behaviour of obese humans and rats to see if there were any other similarities.

In a review of a range of studies where there was parallel research involving both obese humans and VMH rats, Schachter was able to create a ratio to display the difference in behaviour between (what he now terms) 'fat' and 'normal' subjects.

His fat to normal (F/N) ratio involves dividing the score (amount eaten for example) for the fat subject by the score for the normal subject. Therefore, if the fat subject eats 15 grams of food and the normal subject eats 10 grams of food, the F/N ratio would be 1.5, indicating that the fat subject ate 50 per cent more than the normal subject.

The summary table below shows the similarities between the eating behaviour of fat humans and rats across the following range of conditions:

1. *Good-tasting food* i.e. studies such as those mentioned above where subjects are offered food that has/not been laced with quinine. In this case not.
2. *Bad-tasting food* i.e. as 1. above. In this case food that has been laced with quinine.
3. *Amount of food eaten ad lib* i.e. studies where subjects are free to eat as much as they please.
4. *Number of meals per day* – based on self-reports for humans.
5. *Amount eaten per meal.*
6. *Speed of eating* – noting how much food was eaten in a minute.

The table clearly shows the remarkable similarities between the behaviour of obese humans and VMH rats across a range of categories. In addition Schachter found that the behaviour of these two groups was further paralleled in relation to emotionality and activity. Obese humans and rats have been shown to be more sensitive to emotionally charged situations than do normals, but also appear to be rather less active than normals in situations where active behaviour might be expected. Finally, Schachter conducted his own research to complement that of Miller et al. (1950) and Teitelbaum (1957) to show that like the rats in these studies, obese humans will eat less if they

Table 9.1 Fat to normal ratio of obese humans and VMH rats

Condition	Humans mean F/N	Rats mean F/N
Good-tasting food	1.42	1.45
Bad-tasting food	0.84	0.76
Amount eaten ad lib	1.16	1.19
No. meals per day	0.92	0.85
Amount eaten per meal	1.29	1.34
Speed of eating	1.26	1.28

have to work for their food. Amazingly, Schachter was able to show that only 1 out of 20 obese subjects would eat nuts left out for them if they were still in their shells, whereas 19 out of 20 would eat if they had no shells. The figures for normal subjects showed no such difference, 10 out of 10 with shells, and 9 out of 11 without shells.

Evaluation

Most of the studies presented in this summary are experimental and whilst this may not involve much of a change for most of the rats in the study, it can involve significant changes for the humans involved. As such the humans will be subject to a range of demand characteristics and experimenter effects which could cause them to eat more or less depending on the nature of the effect.

Similarly, there are other variables involved in these studies that may have a confounding effect, in particular the type of foods used. In the first study of eating roast-beef sandwiches were used, certainly something that I would turn my nose up at. In other studies various forms of nuts and crackers are used, which again may be susceptible to individual differences in taste.

The studies of rats have also been undertaken in controlled conditions from the point of the lesion to the point of obesity with all aspects of behaviour reported in between, no such controls are possible with obese humans. They arrive in an already obese state, the experimenter has no knowledge of how they came to achieve this state, were they like this in early childhood, is it a recent phenomenon, or what? As such it is difficult to draw any valid conclusions about the similarity of cause in the behaviour of the humans and rats. Indeed Schachter himself seems a little confused about whether such causal claims should be made, sometimes appearing to suggest that they should, at other times suggesting that they definitely should not.

Summary 3

Stephan C.W., Saito I., Barnett S.M. (1998). Emotional expression in Japan and the United States: the non-monolithic nature of individualism and collectivism. *Journal of Cross-Cultural Psychology*, 29(6), 728(21).

Notes

This study considers the cultural influences on emotional expression, considering some of the research already conducted by Stephan herself and others, and the conflicting issues that have arisen. The starting point is the belief that culture does indeed have some influence, but the desire of the author is to consider these effects in the face of ever-changing cultures and the long-held stereotypes that tend to linger concerning certain national/cultural groups.

Introduction

The distinction between individualism and collectivism is believed to be responsible for a number of differences between cultural groups. This distinction is believed to be particularly evident when comparing 'Eastern' cultures, such as Japan, with 'Western' cultures, such as America. These cultural differences have been noted by a number of researchers investigating their effect on behaviour (Triandis, 1988; Kitayama and Markus, 1995). These cultural differences are believed to have led to an attitude in the 'West' which reinforces ideas of independence and individual achievement, rather than interdependence and the obligation to the group.

Stephan et al. placed these issues of culture in the arena of emotional expression with their consideration of the effect of such attitudes on emotional expression. In particular they were interested to see if there would be differences between the two groups in that:

1. The Americans would feel happier expressing independent emotions and the Japanese happier expressing interdependent emotions.
2. The Japanese would make a greater distinction in expressing emotions toward in-group and out-group members than Americans.
3. The Americans would be happier expressing negative emotions than the Japanese.

Method

One hundred undergraduate students from a university in America were chosen and the same in Japan, with an average age of 20 and an even male/female split. They were asked to rate their anticipated degree of comfort/happiness in expressing a variety of emotions to in-group and out-group members, as well as the frequency and level of independence of these emotions.

A five-section questionnaire was administered which measured the degree of comfort in expressing 44 different emotions in the presence of a family member on a six-point scale, running from extremely comfortable to extremely uncomfortable.

Participants were then asked to rate how pleasant each of the emotions was on a six-point scale, running from extremely pleasant to extremely unpleasant.

Next, a measure of the extent to which the participants rated these emotions as independent/interdependent was measured on a six-point scale, running from extremely probable that it helps you to feel independent to extremely probable that it helps to maintain relations with others.

Finally, a measure was taken of their level of individualism/collectivism on a scale which asked participants to rate themselves out of 10, running from 'doesn't describe me at all' to 'describes me very well'. A mean score for each rating for each participant was obtained by dividing each rating by the number of items in each category.

The complicated package of variation and covariation caused some measurement problems and it is consequently difficult to represent the results as simple figures or mean averages.

On the first measure, participants from the United States felt more comfortable expressing emotions to family members than to strangers whereas participants from Japan did not make this distinction. This is contrary to expectations.

On the second measure, participants from the United States were more comfortable expressing negative emotions than those from Japan. This is in line with expectations.

On the third measure, participants from both countries felt more comfortable expressing interdependent emotions than independent emotions. This is in line with expectations for Japanese participants, but contrary to expectations for United States participants.

Interestingly, on the scores from the final test, intending to show the level of individualism/collectivism of each group, Japanese participants came out as more individualistic than United States participants.

Consequently, the hypotheses are not supported and there appears to be little difference in the comfort in expressing emotions between Japan and USA on the measures taken in this study.

Discussion

The overall purpose of the study was to examine the influence of individualism and collectivism on the expression of emotion in USA and Japan.

Expectations were not supported on two out of the three measures taken, but were supported on the measure of comfort in expressing negative emotions. On this measure United States participants were indeed more comfortable expressing negative emotions. However, all of these measures and their relationship to individualism/collectivism are severely questioned by the finding that, contrary to the popular stereotype, the participants in this study did not easily divide up on the measure of individualism/collectivism. It seems that cultures are significantly more dynamic than has been previously believed and this dynamism may have accounted for the differences found.

Methodological issues concerned the problem of using self-reports and the validity problems that arise relating to the willingness of the participants to report their true feelings.

Further problems arise from the difficulty of measuring individualism/collectivism at the group level as well as at the individual level. The participants chosen from Japan in this study may have been unusually individualistic, particularly as they were students.

Glossary

The first occurrence of these terms is highlighted in **bold** in the main text. An asterisk has been used to indicate that a word or phrase has an entry of its own in this glossary.

acetylcholine. A neurotransmitter* that is released at many brain and peripheral sites.

achievement imagery. Related to the kind of images that are present within a society. McClelland believed this would provide a guide to the achievement motivation of that society.

adipocytes. Fat storage cells.

adipsia. The complete cessation of drinking.

aesthetic needs. The desire to have beautiful and/or artistic items surrounding you.

amygdala. A limbic system* structure that is particularly involved in emotional states.

angiotensin II. A hormone* that is involved in the regulation of body fluid.

anorexia nervosa. The failure to eat enough for one's needs, leading to a significant loss of body weight. Common in adolescent females.

antidiuretic hormone (ADH). A hormone* released from the pituitary gland* that helps to regulate water balance by promoting water up-take in the kidneys.

aphagia. The complete cessation of eating.

arousal. A general term for a state of physiological activation.

autonomic nervous system (ANS). Part of the peripheral nervous system*, involved in maintaining a level of activation.

baroreceptors. Areas of the heart and blood vessels able to detect blood pressure.

behaviourism. A theory that involves learning by association and/or reinforcement*.

being needs. Related to the satisfaction of intrinsic desires, such as self-actualisation*.

Cannon–Bard theory. A central theory of emotion that sees emotional feeling as coming from the brain rather than the periphery.

central nervous system (CNS). The brain and the spinal cord.

cephalic phase hypothesis. Powley's view that hypothalamic lesions cause a change in metabolic activity leading to hyperphagia*.

cerebral cortex. The most important part of the telencephalon region of the forebrain. It is involved in higher cognitive functioning.

cerebrospinal fluid. The liquid surrounding the brain.

cholesystokinin (CCK). A hormone* that is released by the intestines and is thought to act as a satiety* signal.

classical approach to emotions. The view that there are a few basic/pure emotions from which all other emotions develop.

cognitive development. The process of development of thinking in humans and animals.

cognitive labelling theory. A two factor theory of emotion that combines the physiological arousal of the James–Lange theory*, with the cortical processes of the Cannon–Bard theory*.

cognitive processes. The processes involved in thinking and reasoning.

corpus callosum. The connecting band of nerve fibres that join the left and right cerebral hemispheres.

corticosterone. A steroid hormone produced by the adrenal cortex.

deficiency needs. Related to the satisfaction of physiological needs, such as food and drink.

dependence. A state in which a drug is required in order to function normally.

depressant. Any chemical/drug that slows down bodily functions and neural activity.

determinism. The view that all aspects of behaviour are determined by in-born characteristics. Commonly associated with instinct theories such as Darwin and Freud. (The opposite of free will*.)

drive. The physical energy that is believed to be behind motivated behaviour.

drive reduction theory. The view that behaviour is directed towards reducing the unpleasant feelings caused by homeostatic deprivation, rather than fulfilling the desires caused by such deprivation (as suggested by **homeostatic drive theory***).

dual hypothalamic control. The process of the LH* and the VMH* working together to turn eating behaviour on/off as required.

Duchenne smile. A 'true' smile. Duchenne believed that lack of muscle movement indicated a false smile. Movement in this area would indicate genuine pleasure.

electrical stimulation of the brain (ESB). Electrical impulses delivered via electrodes to pleasure centres in the brain, which are stimulated by an animal pressing a bar.

endocrine system. A system of glands responsible for the release of hormones. The system is controlled by a 'master gland' (the pituitary gland*).

euphoria. A feeling of ecstatic happiness.

evolution. A theory of genetic changes in animals through a process of natural selection, by which the physical characteristics that aid survival are passed on.

expectancy theory. A theory of motivated behaviour that suggests we will work harder for a reward.

extracellular fluid. The fluid that lies between the cells.

extrinsic rewards. Rewards that are external to the individual, i.e. they come from outside (money), rather than inside (satisfaction).

facial feedback hypothesis. The view that your emotional state is determined by your facial expression and the facial expressions of others.

fight or flight. A state in which an organism has to decide either to fight an opponent or run away.

fluid regulation. The process by which the body maintains a balance of the required fluids in the body.

free will. The view that all aspects of behaviour are controlled by individual actions. Usually associated with humanistic theory. (The opposite of determinism*.)

genetics. The (study of the) influence of genes upon an organism's development and behaviour.

glucostatic theory. The view that the level of glucose in the body is critical in the regulation of food intake*.

goal-setting theory. Locke's view that motivation at work is facilitated by the setting and achievement of realistic goals.

grand theory. A theory that provides an explanation for all aspects of behaviour.

hippocampus. A structure of the limbic system* involved in memory and emotion.

homeostasis. The maintenance of a stable internal physiological environment.

homeostatic drive theory. The view that behaviour is directed by the biological need to maintain a stable internal physiological environment.

hormone. A chemical released from glands that helps to regulate the internal environment.

hunger pangs. Painful feelings in the stomach caused by contractions of the stomach wall. This occurs when the stomach is empty.

hyperphagia. Over-eating.

hypertonic. Refers to a solution that is more concentrated in solutes than some other fluid.

hypothalamus. A part of the diencephalon region of the forebrain. It controls the release of hormones from the pituitary gland* and other homeostatic functions.

hypotonic. Refers to a solution that is less concentrated in solutes than some other fluid.

ideal self-image. The image of the perfect 'self' that people desire to be.

impression management. The process of trying to present a favourable image to others in order to create a good impression of one.

incentive. An external force that is believed to motivate our behaviour.

instinct. An innate (in-born) tendency to behave in a particular way. Usually associated with Darwin and Freud.

insulin. A hormone* released from the pancreas that helps the body to store excess energy sources as fat.

interstitial fluid. The fluid in which the cells are bathed.

intracellular fluid. The fluid inside a cell.

intrinsic rewards. The feeling of reward that comes from inside (satisfaction).

isotonic. Refers to a solution that contains equal concentrations of solutes and another fluid.

James–Lange theory. The view that emotional feeling is based on feedback from the ANS*.

Kluver–Bucy syndrome. A disorder involving behavioural changes (fearlessness and hypersexuality) observed in monkeys after removal of the temporal lobes.

Korsakoff's syndrome. A severe impairment in memory caused by prolonged and heavy use of alcohol.

lateral hypothalamus (LH). An area of the hypothalamus involved in the mechanisms of hunger. Lesions* in this area lead to aphagia*.

learning theory. A theory that attempts to explain how new information is stored and learned. Closely connected to behaviourism*.

lesions. Damage caused to small areas of the brain.

limbic system. A system of forebrain structures that includes the amygdala* and the hippocampus*. It is involved in the process of emotion.

lipids. Fats and related substances such as cholesterol.

lipogenesis. The body's tendency to produce fat.

lipolysis. The body's tendency to release fat into the bloodstream.

lipostatic theory. The view that the content and storage of fat cells is critical in the regulation of food intake*.

median preoptic nucleus. An area of the hypothalamus involved in the control of drinking. It is responsible for the release of ADH*.

mesotelencephalic dopamine system. A system of dopamine producing neurons that extend into the telencephalon area of the brain.

metabolism. The utilisation of energy.

metamotivational states. Not in themselves motivational, but they determine a pattern of motivated behaviour.

need. A physical or psychological desire for something e.g. the need for food or the need for achievement.

negative feedback system. Systems in which the feedback from changes in one direction bring about changes in the opposite direction to compensate.

neurons. Cells that are the basic unit of the nervous system. They respond to electrical activation in the form of nerve impulses.

neurotransmitter. A chemical that is released along the synapses to send activating messages from one neuron to another.

obesity. A substantial increase in body weight caused by eating more than one's needs.

opponent process theory. Solomon and Corbit's view that behaviour is motivated by a desire to reduce pain and increase pleasure.

optimal level of arousal theory. A theory that suggests that all individuals have a different level of arousal that they must strive to achieve.

osmoreceptors. Neurons in the hypothalamus* that are sensitive to changes in osmotic pressure*.

osmosis. The movement of water molecules from hypotonic to hypertonic solutions through a membrane.

osmotic pressure. The pressure that builds up when the concentration of a solution is either too high or too low in salts.

osmotic thirst. Related to the concentration of salts in the body, causing osmoreceptors* to be stimulated, leading to water being drawn in/out of the fluid compartments.

Parkinson's four-factor theory. An explanation of emotion which combines all four factors involved in emotional experience to explain emotional reaction.

performance-related pay (PRP). Payment for work that is related to the successful completion of an activity. Usually in the form of bonuses.

peripheral nervous system (PNS). The part of the nervous system outside of the brain and the spinal cord. It consists of the somatic and autonomic nervous systems*.

physical dependence theory of addiction. The view that addiction to a drug is caused by the body's inability to function normally without it.

pituitary gland. The 'master gland' of the endocrine system. It is responsible for the release of hormones (under hypothalamic control) from peripheral glands.

polygraph test. A test of the truthfulness of a person's responses through the measurement of changes in the autonomic nervous system*.

positive incentive theory. The view that certain behaviours have beneficial characteristics that produce a tendency to continue that behaviour.

preoptic nucleus. An area of the hypothalamus* that contains osmoreceptors*.

primary reinforcers. Reinforcement that comes in the form of items that fulfil basic physical needs (food).

projective test. A diagnostic psychological test that is used (by psychotherapists) to uncover hidden feelings and motives.

raphe nuclei. Part of the brain stem involved in sleep and drinking.

reductionism. The tendency to 'reduce' all aspects of human behaviour to one factor, such as genes or the environment.

regulation of body weight. The process of maintaining body weight at either a set point* or a settling point*.

regulation of food intake. The process of maintaining a stable level of food ingestion.

reinforcement. A part of the learning process which increases the likelihood of future responses. It may be positive (pleasant) or negative (unpleasant).

reticular formation. A network of neurons in the brain stem involved in maintaining the arousal of the brain and the spinal cord.

ritualised aggression. Patterns of behaviour associated with conflict situations.

satiety. Totally full up (with food/drink).

secondary reinforcers. Reinforcement that comes in the form of items that can be exchanged for primary reinforcers* (money).

self-actualisation. The fulfilment of one's potential.

sensation seekers. Individuals who have a greater desire for arousal than most others. They will engage in *extremely* dangerous activities/sports.

sensory deprivation. Being deprived of the possibility of any stimulation through any of the senses.

septal area. A structure of the limbic system* that is (according to Papez) involved in the feeling of emotion.

set point. A level that must be maintained before a mechanism is triggered into action e.g. a temperature setting on a thermostat.

settling-point hypothesis. The belief that the levels (such as fat or body weight) are not set, but are influenced by various factors that lead to a state of equilibrium.

sham feeding/drinking. Food and drink are given to animals (in experimental situations), but instead of going into the stomach it leaves the body through a tube.

sham rage. The undirected aggressive behaviour of animals that have had their cortex removed.

socialisation. The process of learning the culture (norms and values) of one's society.

spontaneous drinking. Drinking through habit rather than need.

stimulant. Any chemical/drug that speeds up/stimulates neural activity.

subfornical organ (SFO). A ventricular organ that is sensitive to angiotensin II*. It helps to control volumetric thirst.

testosterone. The main androgen hormone* produced mainly in the testes.

thalamus. A structure of the diencephalon in the forebrain that is involved in sensory processes, such as arousal.

tolerance. Decreased sensitivity to the effects of a drug following repeated use.

vagus nerve. A nerve that carries messages to and from the heart and the brain.

ventromedial hypothalamus (VMH). An area of the hypothalamus* involved in the mechanism of hunger. Lesions* to this area lead to hyperphagia*.

volumetric thirst. Related to a reduction in blood volume, which brings about a need for water.

withdrawal. Adverse effects experienced after stopping taking a drug to which tolerance has built up.

Yerkes–Dodson law. The view that performance gradually increases with a corresponding increase in arousal, until an optimal point is reached, after which performance gradually decreases with corresponding increases in arousal.

References

Anand, B.K. and Brobeck, J.R. (1951) Localization of a 'feeding center' in the hypothalamus of the rat. *Proceedings of the Society for Experimental Biology and Medicine*, 77, 323–324.

Antin, J., Gibbs, J. and Smith, G.P. (1978) Intestinal satiety requires pregastric food stimulation. *Physiology and Behaviour*, 20, 67–70.

Apter, M.J. (1982) *The Experience of Motivation*. London: Academic Press.

Archer, J. (1991) The influence of testosterone on human aggression. *British Journal of Psychology*, 82, 1–28.

Atkinson, J.W. (1964) *An Introduction to Motivation*. Princeton, NJ: Van Nostrand.

Ax, A.F. (1953) The physiological differentiation between fear and anger in humans. *Psychosomatic Medicine*, 15, 433–442.

Bard, P. (1929) The central representation of the sympathetic system. *Archives of Neurology and Psychiatry,* 22, 230–246.

Berlyne, D.E. (1960) *Conflict, Arousal and Curiosity*. New York: McGraw-Hill.

Blass, E.M. and Hall, W.G. (1976) Drinking termination; interactions among hydrational, orogastric and behavioural controls in rats. *Psychological Review,* 83, 356–374.

Bolles, R.C. (1979) Toy rats and real rats: non-homeostatic plasticity in drinking. *Behavioural and Brain Science*, 2, 103.

Booth, D.A. (1991) Influences on human food consumption. In D.J. Ramsay and D.A.Booth (eds). *Thirst: Physiological Aspects.* London: Springer Verlag.

Booth, D.A. (1994) *The Psychology of Nutrition.* Bristol, PA: Taylor & Francis.

Brady, J.V. and Nauta, W.J.H. (1953) Subcortical mechanisms in emotional behaviour: Affective changes following septal forebrain lesions in the albino rat. *Journal of Comparative and Physiological Psychology,* 46, 339–346.

Briner, R.B. (1997) Beyond stress and satisfaction: Alternative approaches to understanding psychological well being at work. *Proceedings of the British Psychological Society, Occupational Psychology Conference,* 95–100.

Bruch, H. (1973) *Eating Disorders: Obesity, Anorexia Nervosa and the Person Within.* New York: Basic Books.

Campfield, L.A. and Smith, F.J. (1990) Transient declines in blood glucose signal meal initiation. *International Journal of Obesity,* 14 (supplement 3), 15–33.

Cannon, W.B. (1929) *Bodily Changes in Pain, Hunger, Fear and Rage.* New York: Appleton.

Cannon, W.B. (1931) Again the James–Lange and the thalamic theories of emotions. *Psychological Review,* 38, 281–295.

Cannon, W.B. and Washburn, A.L. (1912) An explanation of hunger. *American Journal of Physiology,* 29, 441–454.

Carlson, N.R. (1977) *Physiology of Behavior,* Boston, MA: Allyn & Bacon.

Chen, N.H. (1993) Dopamine and serotonin release-regulating autoreceptor sensitivity in A9/A10 cell body and terminal areas after withdrawal of rats from continuous infusion of cocaine. *Journal of Pharmacology and Experimental Therapeutics.* 267, 1445–1453.

Cohen, S. and Taylor, L. (1972) *Psychological Survival: The Experience of Long-term Imprisonment.* Harmondsworth: Penguin Books.

Colgan, P.W. (1989) *Animal Motivation.* London: Chapman and Hall.

Cox, J.E. and Powley, T.L. (1981) Prior vagotomy blocks VMH obesity in pair-fed rats. *American Journal of Physiology,* 240, 573–583.

Crowell, C.R., Hinson, R.E. and Siegal, S. (1981) The role of conditional drug responses in tolerance to the hypothermic effects of ethanol. *Psychopharmacology*, 73, 51–54.

Darwin, C.R. (1859) *The Origin of Species by Means of Natural Selection*. London: John Murray.

Darwin, C.R. (1872) *The Expression of the Emotions in Man and Animals*. London: John Murray.

Davis, C.M. (1928) Self-selection of diet by newly weaned infants. *American Journal of Diseases of Childhood*, 36, 651–679.

Decke (1971) cited in, Schachter, S. (1971) Some extraordinary facts about obese humans and rats. *American Psychologist*. 26, 129–144.

Delgado, J.M.R. (1969) *Physical Control of the Mind*. New York: Harper & Row.

Dicker, S.E. and Nunn, J. (1957) The role of antidiuretic hormone during water deprivation in rats. *Journal of Physiology*, 239, 476–482.

Dutton, D.C. and Aron, A.P. (1974) Some evidence for heightened sexual attraction under conditions of high anxiety. *Journal of Personality and Social Psychology,* 30, 510–517.

Ekman, P. and Davidson, R.J. (1993) Voluntary smiling changes regional brain activity. *Psychological Science*, 4, 342–345.

Ekman, P. and Friesen, W.V. (1975) *Unmasking the Face: A Guide to Recognizing Emotions from Facial Clues*. Englewood Cliffs, NJ: Prentice-Hall.

Engell, D. and Hirsch, E. (1991) Environmental and sensory modulation of fluid intake in humans. In D.J. Ramsay and D.A. Booth (eds). *Thirst: Physiological and Psychological Aspects*. London: Springer Verlag.

Evans, P. (1989). *Motivation and Emotion*. London/New York. Routledge.

Eysenck, H.J. (1952) *The Scientific Study of Personality*. London: Routledge & Kegan Paul.

Falk, J.L. (1961) Production of polydipsia in normal rats. *Science*, 133, 195–196.

Falk, J.L. (1969) Conditions producing psychogenic polydipsia in animals. *Annals of the New York Academy of Sciences*, 157, 569–593.

Falk, J.L. (1972) The nature and determinants of adjunctive behaviour.

In R.M. Gilbert and J.D. Keehn (eds) *Schedule Effects: Drugs, Drinking and Aggression*, 148–173. Toronto: University of Toronto Press.

Falk, J.L. (1977) The origins and functions of adjunctive behaviour. *Animal Learning and Behaviour*, 5, 325–335.

Fazey, J. and Hardy, L. (1988) The inverted U hypothesis: a catastrophe for sport psychology? *British Association of Sports Sciences Monography No. 1*. Leeds: The National Coaching Foundation.

Fehr, B. and Russell, J.A. (1984) Concept of emotion viewed from a prototype perspective. *Journal of Experimental Psychology. General*, 113, 464–486.

Fisher, A.E. and Coury, J.N. (1962) Cholinergic tracing of a central neural circuit underlying the thirst drive. *Science*, 138, 691–693.

Fitzsimmons, J.T. and Moore-Gillon, M.J. (1980) Drinking and antidiuresis in response to reductions in venous return in the dog: Neural and endocrine mechanisms. *Journal of Physiology*, 308, 403–416.

Fitzsimmons, J.T. and Simons, B.J. (1969) The effect of drinking in the rat of intravenous infusion of angiotensin, given alone or in combination with other stimuli of thirst. *Journal of Physiology*, 203, 45–47.

Flynn, J.P. (1976) Neural basis of threat and attack. In R.G. Grenell and S. Gabay (eds) *Biological Foundations of Psychiatry*. New York: Raven.

Freud, S. (1922) *Beyond the Pleasure Principle, (authorised translation, 2nd ed.)*. London: Hogarth Press/Institute of Psychoanalysis.

Frijda, N.H. (1986) *The Emotions*. Cambridge: Cambridge University Press.

Frijda, N.H., Kuipers, P. and ter Schure, E. (1989) Relations among emotion, appraisal and emotional action readiness. *Journal of Personality and Social Psychology*, 57, 212–228.

Garfinkel, P.E. and Garner, D.M. (1982). *Anorexia Nervosa: A Multidimensional Perspective*. New York: Brunner/Mazel.

Gill, D.L. and Deeter, T.E. (1988) Development of the SOQ. *Research Quarterly for Exercise and Sport*, 59, 191–202.

Gray, J. and Smith, P.T. (1969) In R.M. Gilbert and N.J. Sutherland (eds). *Animal Discrimination Learning*. London: Academic Press.

Green, S. (1994) *Principles of Biopsychology*. Hove: Lawrence Erlbaum Associates.

Harding, C. and Leshner, A. (1972) The effects of adrenalectomy on the aggressiveness of differently housed mice. *Physiology and Behavior,* 8, 437–440.

Hatton, G. (1976) Nucleus circularis: Is it an osmoreceptor in the brain? *Brain Research Bulletin*, 1, 123–131.

Hebb, D.O. (1955) Drives and the conceptual nervous system. *Psychological Review,* 62, 243–254.

Herzberg, F. (1966) *Work and the Nature of Man.* Cleveland, OH: World Publishing Co.

Hetherington, A.W. and Ranson, S.W. (1940) Hypothalamic lesions and adiposity in the rat. *Anatomical Record*, 78, 149–172.

Hohmann, G.W. (1966) Some effects of spinal cord lesions on experienced emotional feelings. *Psychophysiology*, 3, 143–156.

Hull, C.L. (1943) *Principles of Behavior.* New York: Appleton-Century-Crofts.

Ivancevich, J.M. and McMahon, J.T. (1982) The effects of goal-setting, external feedback, self-generated feedback on outcome variables: A field experiment. *Academy of Management Journal*, 25, 2, 359–372.

James, W. (1884) What is an emotion? *Mind*, 9, 188–205.

James, W. (1890) *The Principles of Psychology.* New York: Henry Holt.

Keesey, R.E. and Powley, T.L. (1975) Hypothalamic regulation of body weight. *American Scientist*, 63, 558–565.

Kiloh, L.G., Gye, R.S., Rushworth, R.G., Bell, D.S. and White, R.T. (1974) Sterotactic amygdaloidotomy for aggressive behavior. *Journal of Neurology, Neurosurgery and Psychiatry*, 37, 437–444.

King, F.A. and Mayer, P.M. (1958) Effects of amygdaloid lesions upon septal hyperemotionality in the rat. *Science*, 128, 655–656.

Kitayama, S. (1991) Impairment of perception by positive and negative effect. *Cognition and Emotion*, 5, 255–274.

Kitayama, S. and Markus, H.R. (1995) A cultural perspective on self-conscious emotions. In J.P. Tangrey and K.W. Fisher (eds). *Shame, Guilt, Embarrassment, and Pride. Empirical Studies of Self-conscious Emotions.* New York: Guilford Press.

Kleinginna, P.R.J. and Kleinginna, A.M. (1981) A categorical list of emotional definitions, with suggestions for a consensual definition. *Motivation and Emotion*, 5, 345–379.

Kluver, H. and Bucy, P.C. (1937) 'Psychic blindness' and other symptoms following bilateral temporal lobectomy in Rhesus monkeys. *American Journal of Physiology*, 119, 352–353.

Kluver, H. and Bucy, P.C. (1939) Preliminary analysis of the temporal lobes in monkeys. *Archives of Neurology and Psychiatry*, 42, 979–1000.

Kolb, B. and Taylor, L. (1981) Affective behavior in patients with localized cortical excisions: Role of lesion site and side. *Science*, 214, 89–99.

Kolb, B. and Taylor, L. (1988) Facial expression and the neocortex. *Society for Neuroscience. Abstracts,* 14, 219.

Koopmans, H.S. (1981) The role of the gastrointestinal tract in the satisfaction of hunger. In L.A. Cioffi, W.B.T. James and T.B. Van Italie (eds). *The Body Weight Regulatory System: Normal and Disturbed Mechanisms.* New York: Raven Press.

Laird, J.D. and Bresler, C. (1992) The process of emotional experience: A self-perception theory. In M.S. Clark (ed.). *Review of Personality and Social Psychology: Emotion,* (vol. 13, 213–234). Newbury Park, CA: Sage.

Laschet, U. (1973) Antiandrogen in the treatment of sex offenders. Mode of action and therapeutic outcome. In J. Zubin and J. Money (eds). *Contemporary Sexual Behavior: Critical Issues in the 1970s.* Baltimore, MD: Johns Hopkins University Press.

Lawler, E.E. (1981) *Pay and Organization Development.* Reading, MA: Addison-Wesley.

Lazarus, R.S. (1984) On the primacy of cognition. *American Psychologist,* 39, 2, 124–129.

Leibowitz, S.F. (1992) Neurochemical-neuroendocrine systems in the brain controlling macronutrient intake and metabolism. *Trends in Neurosciences*, 15, 491–497.

Leshner, A., Walker, W.A., Johnson, A.E., Kelling, J., Kreisler, S. and Svare, B. (1973) Pituitary adrenocortical activity and intermale aggressiveness in isolated mice. *Physiology and Behavior,* 11, 705–711.

Leventhal, H. (1979) A perceptual-motor processing model of emotion. In P. Pliner, K.R. Blankstein and I.M. Spigel (eds). *Perception of Emotion in Self and Others.* New York: Plenum.

Locke, E.A. (1968) Toward a theory of task motivation and incentives. *Organisational Behaviour and Human Performance*, 3 157–189.

Locke, E.A. and Latham, G.P. (1990) *A Theory of Goal-Setting and Task Performance*. Englewood Cliffs: Prentice-Hall.

Locke, E.A., Shaw, K.N., Saari, L.M. and Latham, G.P. (1981) *Goal Setting and Task Performance*. Englewood Cliffs: Prentice-Hall.

Logue, A.W. (1991) *The Psychology of Eating and Drinking: An Introduction*. New York: W.H. Freeman.

Lowe, J. and Carroll, D. (1985) The effects of spinal injury on the intensity of emotional experience. *British Journal of Clinical Psychology*, 24, 135–136.

Lykken, D.T. (1959) The GSR in the detection of guilt. *Journal of Applied Psychology*, 43, 385–388.

MacLean, P.D. (1949) Psychosomatic disease and the 'visceral brain'. Recent developments bearing on the Papez theory of emotion. *Psychosomatic Medicine,* 11, 338–353.

Maranon, G. (1924) Contribution a l'etude de l'action emotive de l'adrenaline. *Revue Francaise d'Endocrinologie*, 2, 301–325.

Markus, H. and Kitayama, S. (1994) The cultural construction of self and emotion. Implications for social behaviour. In S. Kitayama and H. Markus (eds). *Culture and Emotion*. American Psychological Association.

Marlowe, W.B., Mancall, E.L. and Thomas, J.J. (1985) Complete Kluver–Bucy syndrome in man. *Cortex,* 11, 53–59.

Maslow, A.H. (1954) *Motivation and Personality*. New York: Harper.

Maslow, A.H. (1968) *Towards a Psychology of Being*. 2nd ed. New York: Van Nostrand-Reinhold.

Matsumoto, D. (1990) Cultural similarities and differences in display rules. *Motivation and Emotion*, 14, 195–214.

Mayer, J. and Marshall, N.B. (1956) Specificity of gold thioglucose for ventromedial hypothalamic lesions and obesity. *Nature,* 178, 1399–1400.

McClelland, D.C. (1961) *The Achieving Society*. Princeton, NJ: Van Nostrand.

McClelland, D.C., Atkinson, J.W., Clark, R.W. and Lowell, E.J. (1953) *The Achievement Motive*. New York: Appleton Century-Crofts.

McDougall, W. (1908) *An Introduction to Social Psychology*. London: Methuen.

McGregor, D. (1960) *The Human Side of Enterprise*. New York: McGraw-Hill.

McKenna, E.F. (1994). *Business Psychology and Organisational Behaviour. A Student's Handbook* (2nd ed.) Hove: Psychology Press.

Meryman, J.J. (1952) Magnitude of the startle response as a function of hunger and fear. Unpublished doctoral thesis. University of Iowa.

Miller, N.E., Bailey, C.J. and Stevenson, J.A.F. (1950) Decreased 'hunger' but increased food intake resulting from hypothalamic lesions. *Science*, 112, 256–259.

Modigliani, A. (1971) Embarrassment, facework and eye-contact: Testing a theory of embarrassment. *Journal of Personality and Social Psychology*, 17, 15–24.

Monello, L.F. and Mayer, J. (1967) Hunger and satiety sensations in men, women, boys and girls. *American Journal of Clinical Nutrition,* 20, 253–261.

Mook, D.G. (1996) *Motivation: The Organisation of Action.* New York: W.W.Norton.

Nelson, J. and Prosser, C.L. (1981) Intracellular recordings from thermosensitive preoptic neurons. *Science*, 213, 787–789.

Nisbett, R.E. (1968) Taste, deprivation and weight determinants of eating behaviour. *Journal of Personality and Social Psychology*, 10, 107–116.

Nisbett, R.E. (1972) Hunger, obesity and the ventromedial hypothalamus. *Psychological Review,* 79, 433–453.

Ogilvie, B.C. (1968) Psychological consistencies within the personality of high level competitors. *Journal of the American Medical Association*, 205, 780–786.

Olds, J. (1956) Pleasure centers in the brain. *Scientific American*, 195, 105–116.

Olds, J. and Milner, P. (1954) Positive reinforcement produced by electrical stimulation of septal area and other regions of rat brain. *Journal of Comparative and Physiological Psychology,* 47, 419–427.

Oomura, Y., Ono, T., Ooyama, H. and Wagner, M.J. (1969) Glucose and osmosensitive neurones of the rat hypothalamus. *Nature*, 222, 282–284.

Papez, J.W. (1937) A proposed mechanism of emotion. *Archives of Neurology and Psychiatry (Chicago)*, 38, 725–743.

Parkinson, B. (1995) Emotion. In B. Parkinson and A.M. Colman (eds). *Emotion and Motivation*. London/New York: Longman.

Parkinson, B. (1996) Emotions are social. *British Journal of Psychology*, 87, 663–683.

Parkinson, B. and Colman, A.M. (1995) *Emotion and Motivation*. London/New York: Longman.

Peck, J.W. and Blass, E.M. (1975) Localization of thirst and antidiuretic osmoreceptors by intracranial injections in rats. *American Journal of Physiology*, 5, 1501–1509.

Pinel, J.P.J. (1997) *Biopsychology*. 3rd ed. Boston, MA: Allyn & Bacon.

Porter, L.W. and Lawler, E.E. (1968) *Managerial Attitudes and Performance*. Homewood, IL: R.D. Irwin.

Powley, T.L. (1977) The ventromedial hypothalmic syndrome, satiety and the cephallic phase hypothesis. *Psychological Review*, 84, 89-126.

Powley, T.L., Opsahl, C.A., Cox, J.E. and Weingarten, H.P. (1980) The role of the hypothalamus in energy homeostasis. In P.J. Morgane and J. Panksepp (eds). *Handbook of the Hypothalamus – 3A. Behavioural Studies of the Hypothalamus*. New York: Marcel Dekker.

Reisenzein, R. (1983) The Schachter theory of emotion: Two decades later. *Psychological Bulletin*, 94, 239–264.

Robinson, T.E. and Berridge, K.C. (1993) The neural basis of drug craving: an incentive-sensitization theory of addiction. *Brain Research. Brain Research Reviews*. 18, 247–291.

Rodin, J. (1981) Current status of the internal-external hypothesis for obesity: What went wrong. *American Psychologist*, 36,361–372.

Rolls, B.J., Rolls, R.M. and Wood, R.J. (1980) Thirst: The initiation maintenance and termination of drinking. In J.M. Sprague and A.N. Epstein (eds). *Progress in Psychology and Physiological Psychology*. New York: Academic Press.

Rolls, B.J., Rowe, E.A. and Rolls, E.T. (1982) How sensory properties of foods affect human feeding behaviour. *Physiology and Behaviour*, 29, 409–417.

Rolls, B.J., Wood, R.J. and Stevens, R.M. (1978) Effects of palatability on body fluid homeostasis. *Physiology and Behaviour*, 20, 15–19.

Rolls, B.J., Wood, R., Rolls, E.T., Lind, H., Lind, R. and Ledingham, J.G. (1980) Thirst following water deprivation in humans. *American Journal of Physiology*, 239, 476–482.

Rolls, E.T. and Rolls, B.J. (1982) Brain mechanisms involved in feeding. In L.M. Barker (ed.) *The Psychobiology of Human Food Selection*. Westport, CT: AVI.

Rosch, E. (1978) Principles of categorization. In E. Rosch and B.B. Lloyd (eds). *Cognition and Categorization*. Hillsdale, NJ: Lawrence Erlbaum.

Rowland, N. and Nicolaidis, S. (1976) Metering of fluid intake and determinants of ad libitum drinking in rats. *American Journal of Physiology*, 231, 1–8.

Russek, M. (1971) Hepatic receptors and neurophysiological mechanisms in controlling feeding behaviour. In S. Ehrenpreis (ed.). *Neurosciences Research, Volume 4*. New York: Academic Press.

Rutledge, L.L. and Hupka, R.B. (1985) The facial feedback hypothesis: Methodological concerns and new supporting evidence. *Motivation and Emotion*, 9, 219–240.

Sanduik, E., Diener, E. and Larsen, R. (1985) The opponent process theory and affective reactions. *Motivation and Emotion*, 9, 407–418.

Schachter, S. (1971) Some extraordinary facts about obese humans and rats. *American Psychologist*, 26, 129–144.

Schachter, S., Goldman, R. and Gordon, A. (1968) Effects of fear, food deprivation, and obesity on eating. *Journal of Personality and Social Psychology*. 10, 91–97.

Schachter, S. and Singer, J.E. (1962) Cognitive, social and physiological determinants of emotional state. *Psychological Review*, 69, 379–399.

Schwartz, G.E., Weinberger, D.A. and Singer, J.A. (1981) Cardiovascular differentiation of happiness, sadness, anger and fear following imagery and exercise. *Psychosomatic Medicine*, 43, 343–364.

Sheffield, F.D. and Roby, T.B. (1950) Reward value of a non-nutritional sweet taste. *Journal of Comparative and Physiological Psychology*, 43, 471–481.

Silber, K. (1999) *The Physiological Basis of Behaviour*. London/New York: Routledge.

Smith, C.A. and Ellsworth, P.C. (1985) Patterns of cognitive appraisal in emotion. *Journal of Personality and Social Psychology*, 48, 813–838.

Solomon, R.L. (1980) The opponent process theory of acquired motivation: The costs of pleasure and the benefits of pain. *American Psychologist*, 35, 691–712.

Solomon, R. and Corbit, J. (1974) An opponent process theory of motivation. *Psychological Review*, 81, 119–145.

Stephan, C.W., Saito, I. and Barnet, S.M. (1998) Emotional expression in Japan and the United States: the nonmonolithic nature of individualism and collectivism. *Journal of Cross-Cultural Psychology*, 29(6), 728 (21).

Stephan, W.C., Stephan, C.W. and Cabezas de Vargas, M. (1996) Emotional expression in Costa Rica and the United States. *Journal of Cross-Cultural Psychology*, 27, 147–160.

Stricker, E.M. (1972) cited in, Stricker, E.M. (1981) Thirst and sodium appetite after colloid treatment in rats. *Journal of Comparative Physiology and Psychology*. 95, 1–25.

Stricker, E.M. (1978) Hyperphagia. *New England Journal of Medicine*, 298, 1010–1013.

Stricker, E.M. (1990) Homeostatic origins of ingestive behaviour. In E.M. Stricker (ed.). *Neurobiology of Food and Fluid Intake. Handbook of Behavioural Neurobiology*. 45–60, New York: Plenum Press.

Strongman, K.T. (1987) *The Psychology of Emotion*, 3rd ed. Chichester: John Wiley & Sons.

Stunkard, A. and Koch, C. (1964) The interpretation of gastric motility: I. Apparent bias in the reports of hunger by obese persons. *Archives of General Psychiatry*. 11, 74–82.

Teitelbaum, P.H. (1955) Sensory control of hypothalamic hyperphagia. *Journal of Comparative and Physiological Psychology*, 48, 156–163.

Teitelbaum, P. (1957) Random and food-directed activity in hyperphagic and normal rats. *Journal of Comparative and Physiological Psychology*, 50, 480–490.

Teitelbaum, P. and Epstein, A.N. (1962) The lateral hypothalamic syndrome. *Psychological Review*, 69, 74–90.

Toates, F.M. (1981) The control of ingestive behaviour by internal and external factors. A theoretical review. *Appetite*, 2, 35–50.

Toates, F.M. (1986) *Biological Foundations of Behaviour*. Milton Keynes: Open University Press.

Tolman, E.C. (1948) Cognitive maps in rats and man. *Psychological Review*, 55, 189–208.

Triandis, H.C. (1988) Collectivism and individualism: A reconceptualisation of a basic concept in cross-cultural psychology. In G.K. Verma and C. Bangley (eds). *Personality, Attitudes and Cognitions*, 60–95. London: Macmillan.

Triandis, H.C. (1994) *Culture and Social Behaviour*. New York: McGraw-Hill.

Vallins, S. and Ray, A.A. (1967) Effects of cognitive dissonance on avoidance behaviour. *Journal of Personality and Social Psychology*, 7, 345–350.

Vroom, V.H. (1964) *Work and Motivation*. New York: John Wiley & Sons.

Wagner, G., Beauving, L. and Hutchinson, R. (1980) The effects of gonadal hormone manipulations on aggressive target biting in mice. *Aggressive Behaviour,* 6, 1–7.

Wagner, H.L. (1999) *The Psychobiology of Human Motivation*. London/New York: Routledge.

Weingarten, H.P. (1985) Stimulus control of eating: Implications for a two-factor theory of hunger. *Appetite,* 6, 387–401.

Weingarten, H.P., Chang, P.K. and Jarvie, K.R. (1983) Reactivity of normal and VMH lesion rats to quinine adulterated foods. Negative evidence for negative finickiness. *Behavioural Neuroscience*, 97, 221–233.

Wong, R. (2000) *Motivation: A Biobehavioural Approach*. Cambridge: Cambridge University Press.

Wundt, W. (1897) *Outline of Psychology*. Translated by C.H. Judd. Leipzig: Wilhelm Engelmann. (Reprinted Bristol: Thoemmes, 1999). First published in German as Wundt, W. (1896). *Grundriss der Psychologie*. Leipzig: Wilhelm Engelmann.

Yerkes, R.M and Dodson, J.D. (1908) The relationship of strength and stimulus to rapidity of habit formation. *Journal of Comparative Neurology and Psychology*, 18, 459–482.

Zajonc, R.B. (1984) On the primacy of affect. *American Psychologist*, 39, 117–123.

Zuckerman, M. (1978) Actions and occurrences in Kelley's cube. *Journal of Personality and Social Psychology,* 36, 647–656.

Zuckerman, M. (1979) *Sensation Seeking Beyond the Optimal Level of Arousal*. Hillsdale, NJ: Lawrence Erlbaum Associates.

Index